O9-AIE-906

People of Destiny

A Humanities Series

There comes a time,
we know not when,
that marks
the destiny of men.

Joseph Addison Alexander

People of Destiny

FRANK LLOYD WRIGHT

By Kenneth G. Richards

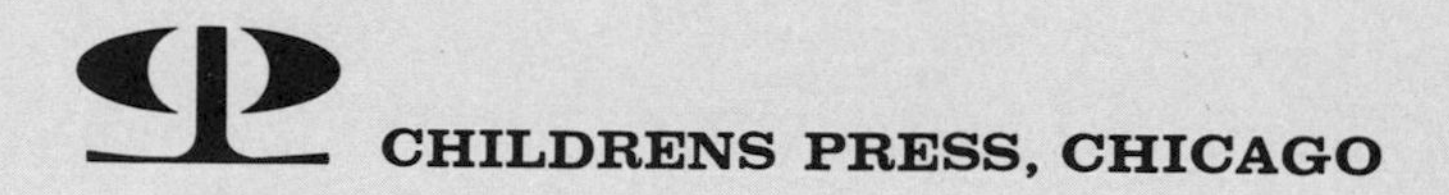

The editors wish to express their appreciation to Mr. Meyer Goldberg, who created the series and inspired the publication of People of Destiny.

Cover and body design: John Hollis

Project editor: Joan Downing

Assistant editor: Elizabeth Rhein

Illustrations: Harley Shelton—Hollis Associates

Research editor: Robert Hendrickson

Photographs: From the files of Wide World Photos, Inc., Hedrich-Blessing, Chicago Architectural Photographing Co., and Historical Pictures Service.

Typesetting: American Typesetting Co.

Printing: Regensteiner Press

Quotations on pages 11, 15, 18, 20, 26, 33, 35, 36, 38, 43, 45, 46, 47, 48, 50, 55, 56, 58, 60, 64, 66, 69, 71, 73, and 89, col. 1, ll. 13-14 from An Autobiography *by Frank Lloyd Wright, by permission of Duell, Sloan and Pearce, affiliate of Meredith Press. Copyright, 1943, by Frank Lloyd Wright.*

Quotations on pages 78 and 89, col. 1, ll. 18-19, 21-22 from Frank Lloyd Wright *by Finis Farr, published by Charles Scribner's Sons, copyright © 1961, by Finis Farr. Reprinted by permission of Brandt & Brandt and Jonathan Cape, Ltd., London.*

Library of Congress Catalog Card No. 68-31305

Contents

An Architecture for America

The twentieth century dawned full of hope and promise. Forward-looking men and women dreamed of marvelous progress for mankind in the years ahead. Great strides were being made in the field of medicine with new techniques in anesthesia and surgery. More and more "horseless carriages" were seen along the streets of the cities. Thomas Edison, C. Francis Jenkins, and others were working on an invention that would make it possible for motion pictures to be shown someday in theaters across the nation. The transmission of voice without the use of wires opened the field of communication to numerous possibilities in the years ahead. Balloons filled with helium, with large baskets attached for passengers, were seen above large cities. There was talk of great airships that would someday carry many passengers—men were even now trying to build a heavier-than-air machine they called the "aeroplane." Yes, there would be great changes during this new century. More technological progress would be made than had been made throughout history.

In only one field—architecture—did men seem to be looking backward rather than forward. New buildings were being constructed every day, the biggest and finest of which are still standing as reminders of past generations who wished to leave a legacy of beauty and culture. Their idea of beauty in architecture, however, was the architecture of the ancient Greeks or Romans, or the style called Gothic which arose in Europe during the Middle Ages.

The designs of many American schools of higher education were based on those of the great universities of the Old World. Many American government buildings bore the unmistakable lines of classic Greek architecture. Magnificent new churches carried the buttresses, pointed arches, and spires of the Gothic period. Romanesque, Byzantine, and Moorish ornamentation and facades concealed modern implements of man—telephones, electricity, and elevators. The architects of some buildings seemed to feel that as long as the design was old, it was good. Consistent use of a single style in a building gave way to *eclecticism*—a mixture of several styles—sometimes to good effect but more often with lamentable results. But for the date on the cornerstone, there is nothing to connect turn-of-the-century buildings with the era of their construction.

One voice cried out for a new concept in architecture. One man was making a serious, concerted effort to bring to America a new style, a new idea, a new truth—an architecture suited to the terrain and temperament of America. "Radical!" and "Rebel!" the establishment called him. But he had a motto "Truth Against the World"—and he was undeterred in his quest for a new form. His name was Frank Lloyd Wright.

FRANK
LLOYD
WRIGHT
ARCHITECT

"Where architecture, as essentially human, once expressed former civilizations," he complained, "our architecture finds popular expression as systems of eclectic 'taste' in imitation."

In his little studio on Chicago Avenue in Oak Park, Illinois, Frank Lloyd Wright began his lifelong crusade to bring a modern style of architecture to America. In this quiet suburb of Chicago he created designs that would at first capture the imagination of only a few liberal-minded observers.

The first phase of his revolution was directed against the "box." The interiors of homes, he said, "consisted of boxes beside boxes or inside boxes, called *rooms*. All boxes were inside a complicated outside boxing. Each domestic function was properly box to box." He conceded that "sleeping boxes" for bedrooms were "perhaps all right." Otherwise, he felt, the tiny, square rooms in most houses "implied ancestors familiar with penal institutions."

The living spaces of a home, he felt, should be open—divided by artistic screens or glass to separate areas for activities such as dining, reading, entertaining, or cooking. He also advocated the extensive use of glass to bring the outside indoors. "The sense of interior space must break through to the sunlight and air," he said. Even in his earliest houses he eliminated "scores of unnecessary doors and no end of partitions . . . The house became more free as 'space' and more livable too. Interior spaciousness began to dawn."

Frank Lloyd Wright was indeed a man of vision. He was one of the first to predict the exodus from the cities to the suburban areas. "The eventual city," he said, "will be greatly different from the ancient city or the city of today." He saw, even then, the present-day trend in American cities to replace the tenement block with high-rise apartment buildings separated by lawns and parks.

He planned the ideal suburb, which he called "Broadacre City," a spread-out community with shopping centers and small neighborhood schools. In Broadacre City, each house was to have an acre of land to provide a sense of privacy. Traditionalists scoffed, of course, but tracts modeled on Broadacre City have sprung up all over America, though the plots of land are usually less than an acre.

Frank Lloyd Wright spent nearly two thirds of this century fighting for the principles and ideals he so deeply believed in. As he persisted in his struggle to change the face of American architecture, his movement gathered increasing numbers of disciples. He had a natural appeal for the youth of America, and the young architects who first took up his cause many years ago dedicated their work to his concepts.

We have only to look around us today to see and understand the genius of Frank Lloyd Wright. Magnificent buildings of glass, steel, and aluminum prove the truth of his ideas. Comfortable homes with picture windows, bright patios, and open living areas owe their existence, in large part, to concepts he championed many years ago. Now, at the beginning of the Space Age, the American people have a style of their own—distinctive, unique, and unprecedented. In the years ahead this style will be referred to as "twentieth-century architecture." The destiny of its earliest champion, Frank Lloyd Wright, has been fulfilled.

For twenty years, from 1890 to 1910, Frank Lloyd Wright lived in this house on Chicago Avenue in Oak Park, Illinois. During this time he designed some of his best prairie houses, including the Winslow, Coonley, and Willits houses.

Truth Against the World

Wales is a stern land. Low, craggy mountains dominate almost all of its roughhewn landscape. Its heather-covered hills are alternately whipped by Atlantic storms or frozen white by Arctic air cascading down from Iceland. A verdant green covers the flinty soil of the narrow Welsh valleys where little fields of crops are anxiously cultivated by stubborn farmers. There is beauty in Wales, a stark, primitive beauty reflected in the indomitable spirit of its people.

This ancient land breeds a strong and independent race of men. From its mines and quarries, from its rock-strewn fields, and from its cliff-faced harbors the Welsh for centuries have earned a meager livelihood. Despite the union with England in the sixteenth century, the hardy, proud men and women of Wales have maintained a strong sense of national pride. The Welsh language still survives, as do many almost unpronounceable Welsh names such as "Rhosllanerchrugog" and "Ystradgynlais." This tiny land of stubborn, proud, resourceful people is the ancestral home of Frank Lloyd Wright.

During the decade just before the American Civil War, a Welsh hatmaker by the name of Richard Jones migrated with his family to America. While still in Wales, Richard Jones had married a lovely, dark-eyed girl named Mary Lloyd. As is sometimes the custom with European families, the names of both husband and wife were combined to make a new family name. The family name of Mary and Richard became Lloyd-Jones.

Mary's family had frowned upon the marriage, for Richard was not only a hatmaker but also a preacher of the Unitarian faith. Because most of his

Mary and Richard Lloyd-Jones, with their eleven children, settled near Spring Green, Wisconsin. Though the family had to work very hard to establish a farm, the bountiful harvest was well worth the effort.

friends and neighbors condemned Richard for his liberal views about religion, he and his family were frequently the butt of jibes and jeers. But Richard was a strong-willed Welshman with deep and unshakable convictions. He upheld his family motto, "Truth Against the World." He would not change. Instead, he decided to take his family and migrate to America with its promise of religious freedom. With their seven children, the dedicated Unitarian preacher and his faithful wife made the harrowing journey to the New World and a new life.

In the pre-Civil War years, Wisconsin was virtually the western frontier of America. It was here, in the small community of Ixonia, that the Lloyd-Jones family first settled. Four more children were born to Mary and Richard while they lived in Ixonia. The family then moved to a quiet valley among the rolling hills near the Wisconsin River. Here, near the little village of Spring Green, the Lloyd-Jones family settled down to farm the virgin Wisconsin soil. The man who had been a hatter and a Unitarian preacher now became a tireless pioneer farmer.

The family prospered, and as the older boys grew up and married, they built their own farms on the surrounding hills above "The Valley," as they came to call it. Some of the daughters grew up to become teachers and one son, Jenkin, became a Unitarian minister. Soon there were grandchildren scampering over the fields and meadows of The Valley. From their fathers and from their Grandfather Lloyd-Jones they learned the lessons of hard, honest work and shared the rewards of a bountiful

harvest. They learned, too, the teachings of the Bible as interpreted and preached by their bearded grandfather.

Anna Lloyd-Jones was the fourth child of Richard and Mary. Only a little girl when the family arrived in Wisconsin, she grew to be a lovely young woman. As a schoolteacher, Anna was called to teach in several of the one-room country schools in the area. She often rode a horse between the school and the homestead, sometimes through the drifting snows of a Wisconsin winter.

Riding alone along desolate country roads would have frightened many young women. But Anna was a Lloyd-Jones—brave, strong-willed, and sure of her convictions. From her parents—and from the family motto, "Truth Against the World"—she had learned the value of education. She believed that truth is of the greatest importance and that truth cannot be found in ignorance.

When Anna was in her late twenties, a traveling music teacher came to Spring Green. He was William Wright, a widower in his middle forties. Anna became enchanted with this dynamic, cultured man from New England. He had been educated at Amherst College in Massachusetts and had worked or studied in many fields—law, medicine, and now music. Despite the seventeen-year difference in their ages, Anna and William were married not long after the Civil War had ended. Her family gave the marriage their blessings.

On June 8, 1869, in the same year that General Ulysses S. Grant became President of the United States, Frank Lloyd Wright was born in Richland Center, Wisconsin. Two years later another child was born to Anna and William, this time a girl whom they named Jane after Anna's sister. In 1872, after William Wright had become a preacher in addition to his other endeavors, he was offered the ministry of a Baptist church at Weymouth, Massachusetts. With hope for the future, but some sadness at leaving the lovely hills of Wisconsin, the family moved to the East.

Pastor Wright was furnished a small, clapboard house next to the old brick church of his pastorate. Ministers of small churches in that era received a very small income, and Pastor Wright was no exception. Members of his congregation occasionally held donation parties to which they would bring offerings of food for the Wright family. These were not well planned, however, and Frank could recall in later years one party that yielded twenty-three pumpkin pies and nothing else!

Quiet, frugal Anna somehow managed to feed the children a healthy diet. Dessert was a rare thing at the Wrights' table, and then only a ginger cookie or gingerbread. There was an occasional pie made from apples sent by Anna's family in Wisconsin. But though the food was not fancy, it was hearty and wholesome and the children grew strong and sturdy. The third child, a daughter, was born in Weymouth and was named Maginel.

Frank led a sheltered existence during the first dozen years of his life. As a minister's son, he attended a private school with most of the wealthy children of the town, and he was admitted at no charge since his father could not afford the tuition. Much to the boy's chagrin, he was forced to wear his hair in long curls, the fashion for wealthy children of the day. This did not prevent him from getting involved in boyish pranks, however, and on more than one occasion he did battle with other boys who taunted him about his hair.

Frank inherited an acute sense of proportion and design from his mother. Despite the family's meager resources, the Wrights' home was a model of simple and tasteful interior decoration. Anna encouraged Frank's instinctive interest in shapes and lines. On occasional trips to Cape Cod or on picnics at nearby churches, Anna helped Frank search out uniquely shaped stones for the collection he was making. She also inspired him to develop a neat and crisp drawing style with his treasured colored pencils.

Frank and his mother work with the Froebel blocks, created to teach children about design, form, and color. In later years, Frank would attribute much of his basic sense of design to the many hours he spent with the Froebel blocks.

In 1876, when Frank was seven years old, Anna made a trip to the Philadelphia Exposition. It was here that she discovered an item which was to have a significant influence on the future life of her son. A man called Friedrich Froebel had designed an unusual set of toy blocks to be used in teaching children the basics of design, form, and color. The set included blocks made in many shapes—cubes, triangles, cylinders—plus strings, small sticks, and balls, all in vivid colors. For an imaginative child, the possible combinations of design were nearly unlimited. Though the set was expensive, as toys go, Anna decided that Frank must have one to sharpen his interest and challenge his progress in learning the fundamentals of design.

Upon her return to Weymouth, Anna began showing Frank the possible uses of the Froebel blocks. In the evening, when dinner was over and Pastor Wright was working on his next sermon, Anna and Frank would sit by the hour building designs according to the instructions that came with the set. Soon Frank was making his own creations as he experimented and developed a sense of design "which never afterward leaves the fingers; so *form* becomes *feeling*."

These years spent in Massachusetts were formative years for Frank Lloyd Wright. They were also historic years for the United States. The western frontier was gradually being pushed farther and farther toward the Pacific Ocean. Railroads were extended to the Mississippi and beyond, making transcontinental travel almost a reality. The first intercity telephone lines were strung between Boston and Salem, Massachusetts.

As the 1870's ended, a chapter in the life of Frank Lloyd Wright came to a close. In 1880, William Wright gave up his pastorate in Weymouth and returned with his family to Wisconsin. But during the years in Weymouth, through his mother's guidance and his own initiative, an idea had been planted in the mind of Frank Lloyd Wright.

Adding Tired to Tired

William Wright settled his family in Madison, the thriving capital city of Wisconsin. Music was the field he loved best, and he gave up having a church of his own to open a conservatory of music where his pupils were mostly Madison schoolchildren. He did continue to preach occasionally at churches in the area. Financially, the Wrights were hardly better off in Madison than they had been in Weymouth. Anna was happier there, however, because The Valley and the Lloyd-Jones clan were only forty miles away.

Young Frank was also pleased with his new home, for no longer did he have to wear the hated curls. As soon as the family arrived, he was taken to a barbershop where his long hair was clipped away. For Frank, who was about to enter his teens, this one trip to the barbershop was almost as good for him as the Froebel gifts his mother had bought for him four years earlier. No longer would he have to worry about teasing remarks from other boys.

When summer came to Wisconsin, Frank was sent to live and work on the farm owned by his Uncle James. Here he learned to apply the Lloyd-Jones philosophy of hard work. Richard Lloyd-Jones had impressed upon his children this lesson: "add tired to tired and add it again." The results of the application of this rule lay in the magnificent farms that sprawled across the valley and latticed the hillsides. It was to be a long, difficult summer for the artistic young man from Madison, but he would learn to love the state in which he had been born.

On his first morning at Uncle James' farm, Frank heard a distant voice through the deep haze of sleep.

"Get up, Frank," the voice called, "it's four o'clock."

Gradually the boy shook himself awake, rubbed his eyes, and stared out of the window. It was still pitch-dark outside! What on earth would Uncle James want at this time of night, he wondered? Again the voice called and

Uncle James Lloyd-Jones awakens Frank once again for another long day of work on the farm. By the end of the summer, though, Frank would even enjoy getting up at dawn and would no longer mind the strenuous farm labor.

this time Frank answered that he was getting up.

Fumbling around in the dark, he managed to find his clothes and shoes, get dressed, and grope his way down the stairs. When he entered the kitchen, which was lighted by a kerosene lamp, Frank stared questioningly at his uncle.

"This is the time we start to work here on the farm," Uncle James grinned. Then pointing to a bucket of cold water on a table near the sink, he said, "Freshen up a bit and then we'll go out to the barn."

The ice-cold water from the deep well shocked the boy completely awake and, donning a broad-brimmed straw hat, he followed Uncle James across the barnyard. Now the boy, who had attended private school in Massachusetts, had his first lesson in milking a cow. Seated on a little three-legged milking stool, with a kerosene lantern nearby, Frank watched his uncle demonstrate the procedure. When Frank tried it himself it seemed like fun at first, but he soon learned that milking requires very strong hands. He strained and pulled with all his might until he was sure the cow was dry—only to be amazed when his uncle's sure, strong hands managed yet another quarter-bucket of milk from the cow. The boy was relieved when Uncle James said it was time for breakfast.

By the time he was scrubbed and seated at the breakfast table, Frank was very hungry. He was served a hearty meal such as he had never known at home. There were ham and potatoes, pancakes and molasses, fresh-baked cornbread, and buttermilk and cheese. Frank pitched into the food with a will but found that his hands ached so that he could barely hold his fork. But he managed, and when the meal was over, Frank eagerly followed his uncle out to begin the day's work.

By now the sun was shining brightly in the eastern sky and the air was beginning to stir. Scents and smells that were strange to the nostrils of Frank Wright filled the morning air. The barnyard odors mingled with the dewy fragrance of the flowers growing near the house. A cold, gurgling stream bubbled through the valley and at the end of the valley Frank could see the broad expanse of the Wisconsin River. The boy from Madison stretched luxuriously and breathed deeply of the scented air. Wisconsin, he decided, was the place for him. And then he set to work.

Frank had never realized the extent and variety of jobs to be done on a farm. There was hoeing to be done, weeds to be pulled, stock and chickens to be fed, barns and coops to be cleaned, fences to be repaired, cordwood to be cut and split, and orchards to be tended. There was a never-ending series of toilsome duties.

The noonday meal provided a brief respite from the day's labors, and once again the table was heaped with good food. Frank ate as much as he could, and then it was back to work again under a blazing afternoon sun. Ax and hoe handles blistered Frank's already aching hands, which were accustomed only to writing and drawing.

Frank thought the day would never end, but finally, in the late afternoon, Uncle James told his nephew and the hired men to put away their tools. Cold water from the well sloshed on his sunreddened face revived the exhausted novice farmer. A home-prepared balm for his torn and bleeding hands helped a little, too. Supper was as lavish as the other meals had been, but now Frank was too tired to eat much. He looked forward to an evening of complete relaxation. But when the meal was finished, Uncle James said, "Time to get the cows home for evening milking."

Frank was stunned. He almost wanted to cry. But he bravely forced his aching legs to carry him to the barn and through force of sheer willpower milked as best he could with his sore hands. Then at long last, as the sun became a fiery ball on the western horizon, he said good night to his aunt and uncle and dragged his aching body up the stairs to his attic room. It was not yet eight o'clock but he carefully lay down on his bed and immediately fell sound asleep without even taking off his clothes.

Hardly had he been asleep, it seemed, when his uncle's voice came once again through the predawn darkness. "Time to get up, Frank. It's four o'clock." Another day. More long hours of forcing pain-racked muscles to obey, and making stiff, cracked fingers grasp a hoe handle. This was certainly the meaning of "add tired to tired and add it again." Day followed laborious day and then at last—at long last—it was Sunday.

Sunday in the Lloyd-Jones family was a day of rest, a day of worship. The cows had to be milked and the stock had to be fed, but otherwise it was a carefree day of pleasure and relaxation. At the little family chapel by the crossroads, the Lloyd-Jones clan gathered to offer their thanks to God for their bountiful life. Afterward there was a picnic in a cool grove of firs where a great feast was set out on rough-hewn tables. The cares of farm life were forgotten for a few hours and the day was enjoyed to its fullest. Frank joined in the prayers and hymns, taking pleasure in his first day of rest since coming to the farm.

Monday morning came early and Frank dragged his weary body from the bed to begin another torturous week of

---

This illustration shows some of the farm chores Frank had to do while staying at Uncle James' farm during the summer. Uncle James expected Frank to do as much work as anyone else.

dawn-to-dusk toil. The days dragged by. Sunday seemed such a brief respite from so many days of heavy work. Finally, the boy felt he could stand no more, and in a moment of desperation, threw down his tools and slipped away from the farm.

He wasn't sure where he was going, but he hoped to find his way back to his mother and the quiet little house on Lake Mendota in Madison. Passing other farms, also owned by the Lloyd-Jones family, Frank made his way to the river where he found an old ferry about ready to cross. Tired and frightened, the boy sat down on the gunwales of the boat and dipped his feet in the cool, murky water. Lost in his thoughts and feeling very sorry for himself, he did not hear the footsteps behind him.

"Hello, Frank," a voice said. Startled, the boy turned to find his Uncle Enos standing behind him. His mother's youngest brother was a good friend who had led Frank and his cousins in games at the family picnics. The boy was too surprised to reply immediately. Uncle Enos held out his hand with a kindly smile and said, "Come over on the grass, Frank, and we'll talk things over."

As they sat in the shade of a tree on the riverbank, a flood of tears poured down the boy's cheeks. Frank could control himself no longer, and sobs wracked his body as he tried to tell his problems to his uncle. Enos' strong arm encircled the boy's shoulders and soon Frank regained his composure. Then the man told Frank Wright something he would remember all his life.

"Just keep on when you are sore and tired and stiff and think you're discouraged," Uncle Enos said. "But you never *are* discouraged. No . . . . And by keeping on, still more, and again more, you'll see you can do most anything and never feel it too much . . . . Work is an adventure that makes strong men and finishes weak ones."

It was dusk when the two walked hand in hand back over the sandy country road to Uncle James' farm. Embar-

rassed and ashamed, Frank avoided the glances of his aunt and uncle and climbed the stairs to his room. No one reproached him and he was left alone to his thoughts. It was very late before Frank finally fell asleep.

Stars still had not faded from the sky when the now-familiar voice echoed up the stairs. "It's four o'clock, Frank. Time to get up." In the kitchen, Uncle James greeted the boy with a smile and a pat on the back. Nothing was said of yesterday's episode. Happy at heart once again, and brimming with determination, Frank strode across the barnyard to begin his chores. He would "lick" this business of adding tired to tired and in time, just as Uncle Enos had said, he would not "feel it too much." A crisis had passed in the life of Frank Lloyd Wright. Henceforth, work would indeed become an adventure.

As the weeks passed and he grew stronger, life became easier for young Frank. He began to see the beauty in his surroundings. For the first time, he became aware of and was able to appreciate the colors, shapes, and patterns of the terrain in this rural environment. Delicate wild flowers blended their pastels with the rich golden yellow of the hayfields. Cool brooks and quiet pools reflected the softly waving ferns and the full-leaved branches of overhanging trees at their banks. Cows grazed peacefully in clovered pastures. Even the towering thunderclouds and the lightning that often appeared to fill the humid sky were no longer fearsome to the boy.

With his newfound strength, Frank had the energy to hike through the countryside when the day's work was done. He learned the habits and the hiding places of wild animals. He learned of snakes—the deadly rattler, the swift blue racer, the enormous blacksnake, and the vicious water moccasin. He knew where berry patches grew, and nut trees and wild cherries. He captured frogs, turtles, grasshoppers, and snails—all to be studied and carefully set free. He came to know the birds—their songs, the whirring of their wings, their chirping. Now each day brought new discoveries, new excitement, new adventure.

It was during this summer on the farm that Frank Lloyd Wright realized something that would one day help to earn him a place in the history of American architecture. Nature, he observed, had a way of blending many things into a balanced design. The shapes and colors of nature fitted together in graceful harmony. Making a box with his hands, the boy framed scenes from vantage points around the valley. No matter where he "focused," nature was in perfect balance. An angular outcropping of rock was balanced in his scene by a stately oak tree. Gleaming white birches contrasted with the dark shadows of an evergreen grove. Nothing in nature was out of place.

Only man-made things seemed to spoil the balanced pattern. Garishly painted farm machinery stood out starkly against nature's colors. The tall, cubic farmhouses, round-roofed barns, and cylindrical silos detracted from the symmetry to be found in the natural scene. Frank reasoned that man-made designs should blend with and complement the natural surroundings. Thus, an idea was born in the mind of Frank Lloyd Wright that was to have dramatic impact upon architectural styling in the decades ahead.

When September came, Frank found that he was not nearly as anxious to leave the farm as he had been before his talk with his Uncle Enos. But soon his parents came for him and he returned to Madison and life in the city. During the summer he had painfully "added tired to tired" and now he showed the benefits of his hard work. Frank was a changed young man. He walked with a manly stride on powerful legs. He gripped his father's hand with strength born of milking cows morning and night. Hard, shiny callouses bespoke hours of gripping a hoe or ax. Biceps bulged beneath his white shirt—the first he had worn since spring. His sun-bronzed face beamed with new confidence.

Yes, he had learned to add tired to tired. The lesson would serve him well as he fought to overcome the numerous obstacles on his path to destiny.

After Frank got used to the hard work on the farm, he began to take time to wander around and enjoy the beauty of the Wisconsin landscape. He happened upon the principle of symmetry in nature during one of these walks, and this principle influenced everything he did as an architect.

Frankandrob Enterprises

On his return from the farm, Frank's family greeted him with open arms. His sisters Jane and Maginel smothered him with a flurry of kisses and "oohed" and aahed" at how tall he had grown. To his outward embarrassment (and secret pleasure), the two girls barely let him out of their sight during his first days at home. They clung to him, each to an arm, everywhere he went and waited on him hand and foot as if he were a returning prince. Jane and Maginel were proud of their big brother.

Frank's mother and father both felt pride in their son, but each expressed it differently. William Wright studied his son in a quiet way and found that a man-to-man relationship was beginning between them. The tall, bronzed, young man had matured considerably during his few months on the farm. After supper, while the girls and their mother worked in the kitchen, father and son discussed farming problems. Mr. Wright listened intently as Frank described the daily routine of the past summer. Yes, Mr. Wright decided, Frank Lloyd Wright the child had been left on the farm. A strong young man had returned in his place.

Anna Wright felt a little sadness mingling with her pride as she fussed and bothered over her son. She was reluctant to admit to herself that her children would someday become self-sufficient. But she knew that there comes the inevitable day when a son begins to acquire the traits of a man and loses those of a child, and the relationship of mother and son begins to change. This was happening that autumn of 1881.

A few days after he returned to Madison, Frank began attending high school. Autumn leaves blanketed the ground as Frank walked toward home after his first day of classes. He had decided that it was a good school and he would like it there. He had not made any friends yet, since he was somewhat shy, but he reasoned that this was only the first day. As he walked along a path leading through a small park he noticed a crowd of boys under a grove of oak trees. They were shouting and laughing as they danced around a huge pile of

Frank scares away the bullies who were bothering a crippled boy, using the strength he acquired during the summer on the farm. He and the boy, Robie Lamp, soon became the best of friends.

fallen leaves. As he drew nearer, Frank watched curiously, trying to figure out what was so much fun. Suddenly a boy about his own age emerged from the leaves.

When Frank stepped close to watch, he saw that the boy was crying. The boy, at least, did not find much fun in the game. Then Frank looked more closely. The boy was crippled and unable to stand, and Frank noticed that two of the jeering boys had the lame boy's crutches. Frank was becoming angry at what he saw.

Suddenly three or four of the boys grabbed their victim once again, while the others heaped more leaves on the hapless invalid. This was more than Frank could bear to watch. Throwing down his books, he pushed into the melee and grasped one of the rowdy boys by belt and collar. Then, with the strength he had acquired on his uncle's farm, he tossed the boy as he would a sack of flour into a stack of leaves ten feet away. Frank tossed another in the same manner and had a third boy by the collar when the gang decided to make a hasty retreat. In a towering rage, Frank called after them that the same treatment was in store if they ever bullied the crippled lad again.

Retrieving the crutches, Frank shook the leaves off the boy, and helped him to stand. By now the boy had stopped crying but was still trembling with anger and fear.

"I don't think they'll bother you again," Frank said. "If they do they'll have to answer to me. By the way, what's your name? Mine's Frank Wright."

"Robert Lamp," the boy replied. "My friends call me 'Robie.' Thanks for your help, Frank. Those fellows do that to me several times every school year. In the winter they throw me into a snowbank." Robie studied Frank a moment and broke into a grin as his composure returned. "You sure surprised them," he chuckled. "I'll bet they leave me alone for awhile."

Picking up his school books, Frank walked along with Robie as the boy struggled with his crutches, his legs dragging helplessly. Frank's strength, developed during the previous summer on the farm, had helped him to begin a lasting friendship. From that moment on, the pair would share school-year adventures, hopes, and dreams—and would become involved together in various projects.

As they came to know each other better, they found they had a common interest in many things, one of which was printing. Robie, who knew a great deal about the various styles of type and the processes used in printing, would often explain these to Frank. They studied the various typefaces used by Chicago and Milwaukee newspapers.

Not long after school started, great black headlines appeared on the front pages of the nation's newspapers, "PRESIDENT GARFIELD DIES!" The twentieth President of the United States had been shot by an assassin the previous July and had lingered all these weeks before finally succumbing. Vice-President Chester A. Arthur now assumed the presidency. The boys discussed what sort of headlines *they* might have used if they published a paper. The more they talked, the more determined they became to have a newspaper of their own. And so began the first "Frankandrob" enterprise. Robie's father allowed the boys to set up an old secondhand printing press in his barn. Later in the year, they moved to the basement and during the years ahead they turned out many a bold circular or broadside on subjects that struck their fancy.

During all this time, Anna Wright continued to encourage her son's interest in design and architecture. The Froebel blocks, of course, had long since been put aside as the main object of Frank's artistic interest. Now he studied pictures of buildings and bridges, and drew many designs of his own. He had a growing portfolio of designs—neatly penciled sketches of towering buildings, powerful dams, and graceful bridges. With the curiosity of youth, Frank was fascinated by many things—but more and more, the central interest of his life became architecture.

His high school years passed swiftly. Each summer he worked on the farm, where adding tired to tired became routine. The first week or two were usually hard, for Frank had to revitalize muscles that had become weak during the winter. But soon his hands were toughened, his muscles toned, and his body tanned. He could be found singing heartily as he worked, adding rhythm to the toil and labor of farm life.

Each September, Frank would leave the farm and return home to his family. The winters in Madison were as funfilled as the summers on the farm were toilsome. Though William Wright was a rather remote and distant man, Frank, his mother, and his two sisters made a joyous group as they sang around the piano. Jennie, as sister Jane was now called, was a very good pianist and Frank, his shyness absent among his family, proved to be something of a clown and mimic. As Frank and Jane sang and pantomimed, their mother and Maginel applauded gaily. Frank remembered these moments all his life.

"These evenings were no concerts," Frank recalled in later years. "They were happy riots. No one could tell where laughter left off and singing began. Nor where singing left off and laughter began."

There were also many happy hours spent with Robie Lamp. Both boys loved to read and they frequently exchanged books and discussed the things they read. The two also had inventive

Frank, his two sisters, and their mother were a happy quartet as they sang and laughed around the Wright piano. Frank remembered these times fondly all of his life.

minds and were constantly working on new ideas and building things in the basement of Robie's home. As the idea for a new project popped into their heads—a bobsled, a new style of kite, an iceboat, or even a crossbow—they set to work with paper and pencil, sketching out a design. Then they would decide on the type of materials needed to build their invention. But often the idea ended when the costs were estimated. Sometimes, though, by saving money and by using secondhand or borrowed materials, their schemes were seen through to completion.

In June of 1885, Frank graduated from high school and the following autumn he entered the University of Wisconsin. In the meantime, however, unhappiness had overtaken the Wright family. William Wright's music school had been failing, and as the family's fortunes dimmed, the strain of disillusionment began to tell on Frank's stern and righteous father. At last, Anna and William Wright agreed to separate and Mr. Wright left the family home. His family never saw him again. At the age of sixteen, as he entered the university, Frank Wright was also the head of the family.

Besides attending college, Frank now had to help support the family. He found part-time work in the office of Allen D. Conover, a contractor and civil engineer. Conover was also the dean of the engineering school at the university. Though Frank received only thirty-five dollars a month, it helped him contribute to the support of his family. And, he gained valuable experience as an apprentice civil engineer. Early-morning classes were followed by work in the afternoons at the Conover office. Then Frank would walk home to a meager supper followed by several hours of French, English, analytical geometry, mathematics, and descriptive geometry. Saturdays were spent at the Conover office, which left only Sundays for relaxation. Once again, therefore, Frank was working very hard, in the best Lloyd-Jones tradition.

It was during this period at the university that a tragedy occurred which would remain in Frank's memory all his life. One day as he was passing the old State Capitol Building, he heard a rumble which steadily increased to a thunderous roar. The entire north wing of the building was collapsing! With others, Frank raced to rescue those people who might still be alive under the great pile of rubble. The sight of the people who had been killed, and of the maimed and mangled survivors, sickened young Frank. He spent many sleepless nights trying to erase the scene from his mind. But the disaster taught him an object lesson in the consequences of faulty building construction that he never forgot.

The months rolled slowly by and Frank was becoming more and more

Frank tries his best to rescue people from the old Wisconsin State Capitol Building, whose north wing one day tumbled to the ground. He never forgot the horror of the disaster, and it made him realize the importance of sound building construction.

frustrated. He felt he was gaining little knowledge which would serve him in the future as an architect, since as a university freshman he could not yet take any courses in his chosen field. The practical experience he received at the Conover office was, he thought, of much greater value. He also knew that, despite the small contribution he made each month, sending him to college was a heavy financial burden on his mother. The family lived in virtual poverty despite gifts of produce and other food from the Lloyd-Jones farms in the valley. Frank felt a deep concern for his family's welfare, and at the same time he wanted a more productive form of activity. He needed a new challenge —one in his chosen field of architecture.

Therefore, in the spring of 1887, Frank came to a decision: he would leave the university and get a job in an architect's office in Chicago, Illinois. He did not confide in his mother, for he knew she would object to his plan. Instead, he secretly pawned a fine set of his father's books for a few dollars and put his plan in motion. Without saying good-bye to anyone, he bought a train ticket for Chicago.

On a dark, drizzly day Frank Lloyd Wright, budding architect, left boyhood behind and struck out on his own. With seven dollars in his pocket and hope in his heart, he rode a clattering train to Chicago, to start a new life and to fulfill his destiny.

Alone in Chicago

Frank felt totally lost as he stepped off the train in Chicago. He had no idea where he was going to go in the city or what he was going to do. He had only seven dollars in his pocket and a list of architects' offices where he could apply for a job. The sight of this great metropolis with its thousands of people hurrying along gaslit avenues, made misty by a constant rain that day, sent a shiver through the boy from Wisconsin. No friendly smiles greeted him, no one reached out a helping hand. In all this great mass of humanity, Frank felt more alone than he had ever felt before. He fought down his rising fear and apprehension and joined the stream of bustling people moving along the sidewalks.

Frank wandered rather aimlessly for several hours, peering at the garish signs and billboards, the cluttered alleyways, and the drab buildings. The trolley cars caught his eye, and he hopped aboard one, neither knowing nor caring where it was headed. At the end of the line, he caught another one going in a different direction. As the rain began to fall more heavily, weariness overtook the lonesome lad. Finally, very late, he took a room in an inexpensive hotel.

For awhile Frank lay on the uncomfortable bed listening to the sounds of the city which was to become his adopted home. His ears told him that the crowds had thinned—only the occasional clatter of a wagon and the clip-clip-clop of a horse and carriage echoed in the streets. In the lonely silence of his room, as sleep began to come, he renewed his determination to find a job and make his way in this booming city on the shores of Lake Michigan. Tomorrow would be another day.

An early riser by habit, Frank was out of bed and dressed before the sun had fully risen over Lake Michigan. The

State Street in downtown Chicago, 1889. In this photo we are looking north from Madison Street. All of this hustle and bustle disturbed Frank Wright when he first arrived in Chicago, but after he got a job and got settled, he quickly became accustomed to big city life.

sky had cleared but the sun's rays had not yet penetrated the shadowy canyons between Chicago's tall buildings. Rested and determined, Frank bought a hearty breakfast and set out to find employment.

With youthful optimism he knocked on the door of the first architectural firm on his list. A polite but firm, "Sorry, come back in a few weeks," was the reply to his well-prepared query. The next stop was the same and the next a blunt "No!" Undeterred, but with pangs of doubt gnawing at his determination, he continued to trudge the streets from one company to the next. By day's end he was still without a job. Returning to his hotel he paid seventy-five cents for another night's room rent. The next day, he was sure, would be better.

Chicago in 1887 was the fastest-growing area in the nation, a lusty young giant sprawling south and west from the lakeshore. Only sixteen years earlier, in 1871, the city had been gutted by the great fire which legend says was started when Mrs. O'Leary's cow kicked over a lantern in her barn. Vacant lots, like missing teeth, still remained between the new buildings in the heart of the city. Blackened rubble in these lots told a mute tale of the terrible holocaust the city had suffered. But someday these blanks in the Chicago skyline would be filled with sparkling new skyscrapers. Within the next three years, Chicago would surpass Philadelphia, Pennsylvania, to become the second largest city in America.

Though the many architect's offices in Chicago had plenty of work to keep them busy, Frank still did not have an easy time getting a job. No one wanted a young man without drawing experience. His second day of searching proved as fruitless as the first. At some offices he was given the courtesy of an interview before being turned away. At others, all he received was a curt "No" with a door slammed in his face. Still he could not think of giving up. He would not accept defeat. A third day of trudging from door to door still brought no results. Now Frank was rapidly running out of money. His diet was reduced to doughnuts and bananas—the least expensive food he could find. Tired and discouraged, he returned to his hotel room once more and went to bed—this time with an empty stomach.

Frank knew that the next day, his fourth in Chicago, would be the most critical day of his young life. He pondered the alternatives available if he did not find a job then. His money was almost completely gone. Only a few pennies remained after he had paid his room rent. After buying a doughnut for breakfast, there would be nothing left. Even if he decided to give up and return home, he would have to walk or hitchhike. He knew that his Uncle Jenkin Lloyd-Jones lived in Chicago and, in fact, was having a new church built for his Unitarian ministry. Uncle Jenkin could get him a job somewhere with very little trouble. But Frank also knew he would have to face a personal sermon directed with all the power and fervor for which Uncle Jenkin was famous—and anyway, Frank wanted to get a job on his own merits. No, he would not seek help from Uncle Jenkin. When he at last fell asleep, Frank still had not decided what he would do if his efforts failed the following day. The inborn Lloyd-Jones trait of stubborn courage could not comprehend failure.

In the morning, Frank left his bag with the desk clerk and with a portfolio of his drawings began walking the streets once more. Again the rejections came, but at last his path led him to the offices of J. L. Silsbee—who was the architect of Uncle Jenkin's new church. Even in his desperate circumstances, Frank's pride would not permit him to resort to the use of his uncle's name to help land a job. He refused to mention that he was related to one of the company's best clients. He would apply for this job as he had for the others—completely on his own merits.

In the Silsbee outer office, Frank was greeted by a bearded young man with a pleasant smile and courteous manner.

Frank looked everywhere for a job as a draftsman, but no one wanted a boy without experience in drawing. After three days of this, Frank was almost broke and very hungry, but he refused to give up or to go to his Uncle Jenkin Lloyd-Jones for help.

After introducing himself as Cecil Corwin, a draftsman for Mr. Silsbee, the young man invited Frank to sit down and talk. Corwin did not look over Frank's drawings at first. Instead he studied the young man from Madison as he spoke.

Suddenly Corwin interrupted with a question. "You're a minister's son, aren't you?"

"Why, yes," Frank replied in astonishment, "how did you know?"

"I'm one myself, so I can always tell. So is Silsbee, and (he pointed to the office where other men were working) there are two more in there. If you come in here, there would be five of us."

"Well," said Frank hesitatingly, "*could* I by any chance come in?"

With that, Corwin asked to see Frank's drawings. After he had looked through them, he took them into the office of Mr. Silsbee. In a few minutes, he returned to the anxious young man and said, "Mr. Silsbee says to take you on as a tracer at eight dollars per week. Not much, but better than nothing."

Though he would be making less money than he had earned in his part-time job with Allen Conover, Frank quickly accepted the job, thereby taking his first step into the profession in which he would someday become famous.

Cecil invited Frank to lunch, correctly guessing that Frank was hungry and had no money. Later that afternoon, Frank accepted Cecil's invitation to come and stay at the Corwin home until he could find a permanent place to live. That night, Frank wrote a long letter to his mother and sisters, telling them all that he had been doing for the past five days. Before he mailed it, he enclosed in the envelope a ten-dollar bill Cecil had loaned him. His tenacity had served him well. He now had employment in his chosen field—in spite of the fact that the starting pay was low. He had made a good friend and was living in comfortable quarters—though it was true he could not impose upon the gracious Corwin family too long. He was able to send money back to his mother—even if the money had

been borrowed. To some people, Frank's position would seem tenuous at best. But not to Frank Lloyd Wright. Besides courage and resourcefulness, he also had a large measure of determination and confidence. Though he might have doubted, during those first days in Chicago, that he would ever become an architect, all doubt was banished now. The dream his mother had had since before Frank's birth would come true.

Frank enjoyed his work at the office and came to admire Mr. Silsbee. Many years later he would write, "Silsbee could draw with amazing ease. He drew with soft, deep black lead pencil strokes and he would make remarkable free-hand sketches of that type of dwelling peculiarly his own at the time. His superior talent in design had made him highly respected in Chicago. His work was a picturesque combination of gable, turret and hip with broad porches quietly domestic and gracefully picturesque."

Mr. Silsbee was a rather remote sort of man. He had little to say to any of the lesser help in the office. It was Cecil Corwin who served as the link between Silsbee and the draftsmen. "But I adored Silsbee just the same," Frank wrote. "He had style . . . I learned a good deal about a house from Silsbee by way of Cecil."

Months passed as Frank worked, studied, and learned. Meanwhile, he continued to plan for the day when he could bring his mother and his sister Maginel to live in Chicago. His sister Jennie was now teaching school in Wisconsin.

After three months of working for Silsbee as a tracer, Frank felt that he should be given more responsibility, or at least more money. But Silsbee refused to give Frank a raise, so he abruptly left the office and found a job as a designer with the firm of Beers, Clay and Dutton. He soon realized that the new job was not what it had seemed, and he decided to go back to Silsbee's firm in his old capacity—if they would have him.

The day he returned to Silsbee's was like the day not so long before when he had returned to Uncle James Lloyd-Jones' farm after running away. Very little was said about his departure, but he was welcomed back—and was given the raise in pay that had been one of the reasons for his departure in the first place.

Frank's pay was now eighteen dollars per week, and he was able to send for his family. He found them a place to live in the suburban town of Oak Park.

In this year of 1888, Oak Park, Illinois, was a quiet, small community with broad, oak-lined avenues and fine homes. Because it was ten miles from teeming Chicago, the town could maintain an air of peaceful charm while still having easy access to the city. Otherwise, Oak Park was not noteworthy, but within a decade or so, it would become famous as both the birthplace of the famous author, Ernest Hemingway, and the home of Frank Lloyd Wright.

Frank is shown here with Cecil Corwin, the head draftsman for J. L. Silsbee's firm. Frank got his first job in Chicago here, as a tracer at eight dollars per week. Cecil befriended Frank, knowing that the boy had no money and no place to stay for the night.

The Sullivan Years

One day in 1888, the year Benjamin Harrison defeated Grover Cleveland for the presidency, Frank Lloyd Wright heard a bit of news that was to change his life. From a friend, Frank learned that the firm of Adler and Sullivan was looking for a draftsman. "My heart jumped," he wrote. "I had already formed a high idea of Adler and Sullivan. They were foremost in Chicago." He felt a sense of loyalty to the Silsbee firm, however, since they had taken him back so graciously after his short-lived departure. Before going to apply for the new job he talked things over with his friend and foreman, Cecil Corwin.

"Go on, Frank," Cecil said, "you've got pretty much all there is to get here; Sullivan is the coming man in the West. He may be just what you need. Anyway, no harm to try."

Since Frank knew that Sullivan favored a distinct ornamental styling, he selected some of his own drawings, done in a similar fashion, to show the great architect. Sullivan studied the work, studied the intensely eager young man, and then hired Frank at a starting wage of twenty-five dollars per week. This proved to be a turning point in the life of Frank Lloyd Wright.

Louis Henri Sullivan was a small young man of thirty-two when Frank appeared at his office, but already was noted as one of America's foremost modern architects. He had studied at the Massachusetts Institute of Technology at Cambridge and at the Ecole des Beaux-Arts in Paris. Following this, he had worked in various offices in Philadelphia and Chicago before teaming with the rather remote and distant engineer-architect, Dankmar Adler. Sullivan's slogan, "form follows function," states his theory that architectural styling should derive from and express the function for which the building is designed.

The brightness, the space, and the acoustics of modern classrooms, for example, are the result of modern ideas both in education and construction, coupled with the design of new materials. Nineteenth-century schools, hospitals, and libraries were cramped and poorly lighted boxlike affairs that had not been designed with comfort in mind. Today, each is designed for its own particular function and all are more pleasant buildings to be in. This modern approach is what Louis Sullivan had in mind.

Frank began his association with Sullivan at the time of the architectural revolution in America. This trend was reflected mainly in the design of new large buildings. Louis Sullivan felt that these buildings should express the

---

The photograph at right shows the Transportation Building built for the Columbian Exposition held in Chicago in 1893. The building was designed by the firm of Adler and Sullivan, at the time the best architectural firm in Chicago.

conditions and spirit of the age in which they were designed. He was a leading pioneer of modern architecture, but it lay to his disciple, Frank Lloyd Wright, to go deeper into this theory and make the most decisive, giant strides in this movement.

Sullivan was especially pleased with Frank's ability to understand his wishes and to effectively express them at the drawing board. To the young draftsman, Sullivan became *Lieber Meister* (Dear Master). Admiring Sullivan as he did, Frank worked very hard to emulate his idol "until I could make designs and draw them in his manner so well, that toward the end of his life he would mistake my drawings for his. I became a good pencil in the Master's hand."

Because of the heavy reliance Sullivan placed in Frank almost from the beginning, other draftsmen of the firm took a dislike to the youth, whom they considered an intruder. When Sullivan put Frank in an office by himself, the others grew extremely resentful and began referring to Frank as "Sullivan's toady." So they devised a plan to get rid of this young upstart.

There was a back room in the building where each noon hour the men would don boxing gloves and spar a few rounds. They hoped to entice the unsuspecting "boss's pet" into putting on the gloves for a little sport. Frank, however, knew what they were up to. Any encounter in which he was involved would be anything but sport. But he also knew he would have to fight eventually or they would make life unbearable for him. Accordingly, he managed to postpone the day of reckoning until

he could complete a two-week cram course in boxing techniques at a local gymnasium. Though he never had any doubts as to his stamina and strength, he did know that skill plays a very large part in a boxing match. The office workers he was going to box with had been practicing at lunchtime for months. His instructor at the gym allowed only enough time for him to learn a few basic feints and blocks, and also how to jab a man off balance and then follow with a right cross. After the course was over, Frank felt that he knew enough to take on his co-workers.

Each of the "gang" wanted first crack at Frank. A man named Isbell was chosen. Fortunately for Frank, Isbell was simply a "slugger" with no boxing finesse. A successful slugger must have more strength and power than his opponent. Poor Isbell found out too late that the quiet lad from Madison had far more strength than he and, even worse, was a much better boxer. "Izzy" never had a chance and with a bruised body, reddened face, and bloodied nose, quit after two rounds. Without giving Frank a chance to rest, another man, Billy Gaylord, donned the gloves. Billy, who considered himself a good boxer, danced around, bobbing and weaving and tossing light, flicking jabs at Frank. With that, Frank changed his style, moved in quickly and finally knocked Billy down. That ended the "sport" for that noon.

The ringleader, "Ottie" Ottenheimer, had not been present for the noontime bouts, so the following day he decided to teach Frank a lesson on his own. In a bloody brawl of a fight Frank succeeded in knocking Ottie unconscious. Frank

had never intended that to happen, and alarmed and shaken at what he had done, he helped to revive the stricken bully. He sighed with relief when the man was able to stand again—and watched surprised as Ottie brushed himself off, gathered up his drawing equipment, and walked out the door never to return. After that, no one bothered Frank Wright.

Because city properties at this time were becoming increasingly more expensive, it was necessary to make better use of each plot of land. The invention of the hydraulic elevator made possible the building of tall structures which would require very little land space. Only the year before, the first hydraulic electric elevator had been installed in the Demarest Building in New York City. Adler and Sullivan's major project at the time Frank joined them was the design and construction of the Auditorium building in Chicago. This was an immense undertaking that included an opera house to seat some 4000 people, a four-hundred-room hotel, and space for numerous business offices—partly in a seventeen-story tower with an elevator.

This project, often recognized as Sullivan's greatest, was to occupy most of Frank's time until its completion in 1890. President Benjamin Harrison and Vice-President Levi P. Morton attended the gala opening night performance of the opera in the Auditorium Theatre.

It was to the top floor of the tower in the Auditorium building that Adler and Sullivan moved in 1890. From his new office, Frank could get a spectacular view of the sprawling metropolis. Here the firm's business grew rapidly as commissions were received for an increasingly large number of office buildings and business blocks. There was so much commercial business that very few assignments to build homes could be accepted; the few that were accepted were done by Frank.

Meanwhile, romance was blooming between Frank and a young girl he had met at a church dance held at Uncle Jenkin Lloyd-Jones' All Souls Unitarian Church. Not long after his arrival in Chicago, Frank had begun attending study classes at the church. The classes covered a variety of subjects, not all religious. Included was a study of Victor Hugo's book *Les Miserables.* The reading and discussion of this book took several weeks and when it was finished, the students decided to hold a supper and dance in celebration. It would be a costume ball—each student was to come costumed as a character from the book. Frank was to dress as Enjolras, a French cavalry officer.

Frank cut quite a figure at the celebration, with his crimson jacket trimmed in gold, his tight-fitting white trousers, and his shiny black knee-high boots. For added effect, he had borrowed an immense cavalry sabre in an embossed leather scabbard.

During an intermission, Frank had literally bumped into the girl of his dreams. While crossing the dance floor, he accidentally collided head on with a young lady who wasn't looking where she was going. There was a resounding *thump* and Frank staggered backward as the girl fell to her knees. Quickly regaining his composure, Frank helped the girl to her feet, all the while stammering apologies. The girl was not angry at all, but just rubbed her forehead, laughingly saying it was all her fault. She assured Frank she was quite all right.

Relieved that she was uninjured, Frank really looked at the girl for the first time. She was a tall, slender, strawberry blonde with a lovely face and a dazzling smile. Her costume was that of

---

This photograph is of the Auditorium Building in Chicago, completed in 1890. Frank did a great deal of work on this building as a draftsman for Adler and Sullivan, the firm which designed the building. Many say this building was Louis Sullivan's greatest.

a French peasant girl, with an embroidered bodice and billowing skirt. Frank was as staggered by her beauty as by the collision, but with the aplomb befitting the costume he was dressed in, he escorted her to her parents' table. Her name, he learned, was Catherine Tobin.

Mr. and Mrs. Tobin invited Frank to Sunday dinner the next day and Frank, completely smitten with Kitty, as she was called, readily accepted. Kitty, it turned out, was only sixteen. She appeared to be older, for she was a tall girl and possessed mature common sense. After dinner she and Frank went for a walk through the Kenwood district where the Tobins lived. In time, a serious romance developed between Frank and Kitty. The two young people wanted to be married, but Kitty's parents felt that she was too young to think of marriage. They sent her away to visit relatives in Michigan for awhile, thinking that perhaps there she would soon forget her ardent architect admirer. In this instance, however, absence did indeed make the heart grow fonder. Not long after her return, wedding plans were made.

Louis Sullivan was pleased that his best draftsman was going to marry and settle down, and he offered him a five-year contract, which Frank gratefully accepted. Sullivan then loaned his young apprentice enough money to buy a plot of land in Oak Park and build a small house. Life looked rosy indeed to Frank Lloyd Wright. He was about to marry the girl of his dreams, he had a contract with the foremost architectural firm in Chicago, and he would soon have a home of his own.

In the fall of 1890, twenty-one-year-old Frank Lloyd Wright married seventeen-year-old Catherine Tobin. The wedding ceremony was performed by Uncle Jenkin in his All Souls Unitarian Church. For their honeymoon Frank took his bride to his childhood home at The Valley in Wisconsin. The young couple then returned to Oak Park and their first home.

Frank had built a drafting studio in the little house in Oak Park. It was here that he worked on designs for houses. Adler and Sullivan, of course, had to approve the plans later, but Frank was pretty much on his own in this facet of the firm's activities.

Meanwhile, the Frank Lloyd Wrights were acquiring a family. Within a year after their marriage, Catherine presented Frank with a son, whom they named Lloyd. Two years later another son, John, was born. Coupled with the cost of raising a growing family, the Wrights had begun to develop rather expensive tastes. Frank, however, had rapidly gained a reputation of his own

Frank Lloyd Wright throws down his pencil and walks out of the Adler and Sullivan office as the result of a dispute over Frank's outside work. Though he never went back to work for him, Frank always felt indebted to Louis Sullivan for the invaluable experience he had received in Sullivan's office.

and clients began coming directly to him when they wanted a house designed. He was thus able to increase his income by taking assignments independent of Adler and Sullivan. He executed them in his studio at home, on his own time, but when Mr. Sullivan discovered what Frank was doing he claimed that Frank had broken their contract. Frank, of course, disagreed strongly and in the resulting argument "threw my pencil down on my table and walked out of the Adler and Sullivan office . . . never to return."

So ended a most significant period in the life of Frank Lloyd Wright. The six years of apprenticeship under Louis Sullivan, one of the finest, most progressive architects of his time, had provided Frank with a background of experience probably unattainable anywhere else. Throughout his life, Frank would always refer to Sullivan as Lieber Meister.

Wright now began a career of independent practice that would ultimately result in widespread acclaim of his architectural genius. His career, like those of many geniuses, would be a roller coaster ride to towering pinnacles of fame interspersed with plummeting falls to near oblivion. But Frank Lloyd Wright's path of destiny would lead America and the world to a new concept of architecture.

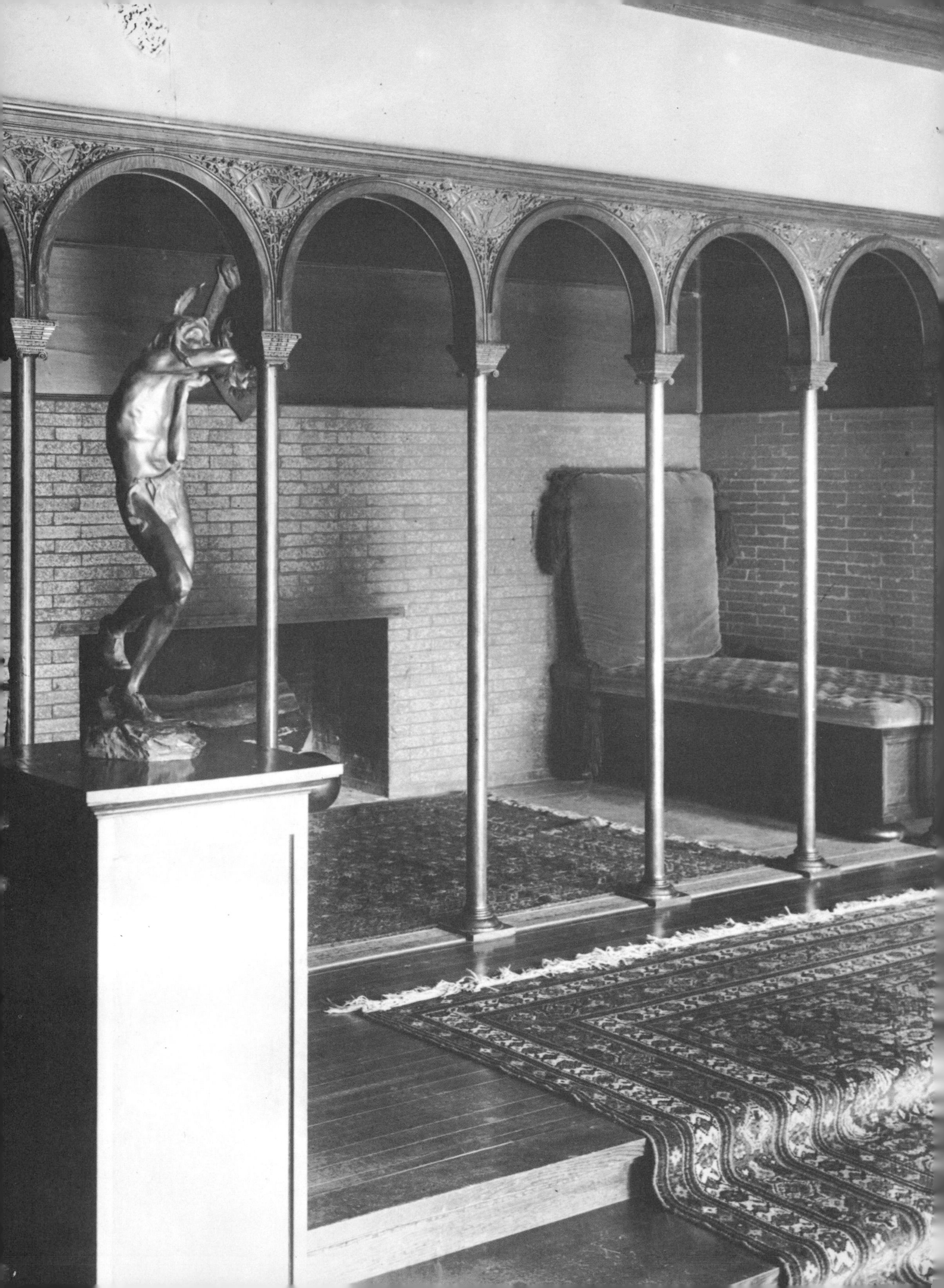

A House for the Prairie

With his old friend Cecil Corwin, Frank opened an office of his own in 1893. Not long afterward, Frank got his first commission as an independent architect. Mr. W. H. Winslow of suburban River Forest, Illinois, asked Frank to design a home for him. The young architect, eager to test his ideas, was delighted with this opportunity. He immediately set to work at his drawing board. The home he designed for Mr. Winslow was the first of Frank Lloyd Wright's "prairie houses." It was to make history in the field of architecture.

Frank had felt an increasing dissatisfaction with the homes in Chicago's suburbs. In later years he would refer in disgust to the typical houses he saw in and around Oak Park. "To take any one of these so-called homes away," he wrote, "would have improved the landscape and cleared the atmosphere. It was a box that had to be cut full of holes to let in light and air and an especially ugly one to get in and out of, or else it was a clumsy 'gabled' chunk of roofed masonry similarly treated."

A house, Frank felt, should have a "sense of unity . . . a sense of space as should belong to a free man among a free people in a free country." In response to this feeling, "A new sense of simplicity as 'organic' had barely begun to take shape in my mind when the Winslow house was planned. But now it began in practice. Organic simplicity might be seen producing significant character in the harmonious order we call nature."

By "organic simplicity," Wright meant that a building should fit into the natural balance of its location. It should be constructed of materials native to the region, it should be free of excessive ornamentation unrelated to its function, and most of all it should "be" a part of the land on which it is built. In applying the idea of organic

---

This photograph is an interior shot of the first house Frank Lloyd Wright designed as an independent architect. after his departure from Adler and Sullivan. The house was commissioned by W. H. Winslow of River Forest, Illinois, and was the first of Frank's prairie houses.

simplicity in architecture to the houses he designed for the prairie landscape of Illinois, Frank arrived at an entirely new concept in American architecture. "I saw that a little height on the prairie was enough to look like much more," he explained. "Every detail as to height becomes intensely significant. I had an idea that the horizontal planes in buildings, those planes parallel to earth, identify themselves with the ground—make the building belong to the ground. I began putting this idea to work."

The Winslow house incorporated many of Frank's ideas. To accentuate the horizontal design, he lowered the roof by not including an attic and did not include a basement. He also designed the home with lower room ceilings than most of the homes of the era had. He strived for an openness within the house, too, and treated the lower living spaces as one room. In place of walls, he used screens to separate the areas to be used for dining, relaxing, and cooking. Today we call screens of this type "room dividers."

The prairie houses had a common feature besides the low, horizontal design. This special feature was a broad, protective eave extending from a gently sloping roof. The undersides of these eaves were painted a light color so that they would reflect light into the upper-story windows. "I liked the sense of shelter in the look of a building," Frank explained. To this day, no design has ever created a greater sense of protectiveness than the Frank Lloyd Wright prairie houses.

When he designed a house, Frank thought in terms of "organic architecture," in which all parts of the house itself—site, exterior, interior, fixtures, and furnishings—presented a continuity of design and function. In other words, each part contributed to and blended with the total design both from a standpoint of beauty and of human use and comfort.

To achieve his distinctive style with its goals of organic simplicity in architecture, Frank discarded many of the traditional methods of architecture. He conceived an idea of architectural "plasticity" which he defined as "the expression of a thought." The achievement of this plasticity required the use of different materials and construction than had been used in architecture before that time.

Traditionally, walls and ceilings simply reflect the skeleton framework of upright posts, horizontal beams, and cornices. With his concept of plasticity in architecture, Frank could "let walls, ceilings, floors become *seen* as component parts of each other, their surfaces flowing into each other to get continuity in the whole . . . "

Public reaction to the Winslow house, and to those that immediately followed it, was mixed. Many people viewed the homes with admiration, while a number of conservative critics heaped ridicule upon both the architect and the homeowners. These critics felt that the exterior of a house should take precedence over all other factors. It didn't matter to them whether the interior was comfortable, as long as the exterior looked like a replica of an ancient or Gothic style of architecture. But regardless of the reaction, Frank Lloyd Wright's houses always attracted a great deal of attention.

Meanwhile, Frank's family continued to grow. By the end of the century, three more children had been added to the Wright clan—Catherine II, David, and Frances. Frank was a tolerant and doting father who delighted in his children and readily joined in their activities and games. "The handsome children were well born," he would later say with pride. "They, each and all, were fine specimens of healthy childhood. They were all curly-headed, blue-eyed, sunny-haired, fair-skinned like their beautiful mother. They all resembled her."

Frank himself seemed to possess unlimited energy. Bright and early each morning he walked briskly to the station to catch the commuter train. He cut quite an imposing figure with his somewhat flamboyant neckties and his sandy-colored hair worn in a distinctive, rather bushy style. After a busy day in Chicago, he would return to the bustling household in Oak Park. "That household was a double-barreled establishment," he remembered in later years, "a three-ring circus." Clients and associates who came to call often found the architect romping on the floor with his brood, or boxing with one of the boys.

When Frank's original studio in the house on Forest Avenue was taken over as a nursery and child's bedroom, a new studio facing Chicago Avenue was built on the lot. This studio eventually became Frank's office and workshop and he no longer had to commute to and from the city. Frank then connected the studio with the house by building a corridor between the two. A tree stood in the way of this corridor, but Frank's love of nature prevented him from cutting it down. Instead, he built the corridor around the tree, to the delight of his children who brought all their friends to see their "house with the tree growing out of it."

In 1896, Frank took on a task which was to have no monetary reward, but would provide him with great satisfaction and pride for all the years of his life. Previously, he had designed a building for his two silver-haired aunts, Nell and Jane, who opened a school on the site of the original Lloyd-Jones homestead in The Valley. With the family motto, "Truth Against the World," as their school creed, the two teachers moved into the completed building, the Hillside Home School, where they began to educate youngsters. When a water reservoir was placed on the hilltop above the school, the aunts needed a windmill erected at the crest. The usual farm windmills were designed strictly for the function they were to perform—that of pumping water. Because no one had ever tried to make the towers attractive, they were stark and functional frames of steel or timbers standing along the hill slopes. This would not do for aunts Nell and Jane. They wanted a "pretty windmill tower in keeping with our school building." They asked Frank to send them a design.

Frank, of course, knew the landscape by heart. Many times he had climbed to the crest of this tallest hill in the area to enjoy the view. Many times from the other nearby valleys he had shaded his eyes against the sun to see this quiet

---

The illustration at right depicts the construction of Tower Romeo and Juliet. This was the windmill tower Frank designed for the Hillside Home School in Wisconsin, run by his aunts Nell and Jane. The tower was revolutionary in that its design was both functional and beautiful.

height where cool breezes always seemed to blow. He agreed with his aunts—that crest should not be crowned with an ugly steel windmill. He set to work with pencil and T square and soon had a unique design which he felt had beauty and yet would stand the howling gales and storms that occasionally lashed the area. He sent the drawings, along with a perspective sketch, to his aunts.

The Lloyd-Jones clan met to discuss Frank's revolutionary design. Frank's five uncles expressed doubt that the tower would stand in a strong wind. They also felt that Frank's tower was not worth the price, since it would be more than three times as expensive as a steel tower. But, despite the opposition of their brothers, the aunts prevailed. They sent a telegram to Frank for reassurance: "ARE YOU SURE IT WILL STAND?" Frank's reply came in two words: "BUILD IT!" And so they did.

The tower was connected to a solid stone foundation with powerful strap bolts. Frank's original design included a heavy, diamond-shaped mast which bore the weight of the great wheel; a knifelike edge of this diamond projected in the direction of the prevailing wind. Frank called this edge a "storm prow." The main body of the tower was octagon shaped, and its heavy timber uprights were sheathed with boards. The exterior was shingled. The tower was designed to sway several inches in the wind, a feature we now know to be necessary in building tall structures. This feature, however, terrified the local workmen who were building the tower and convinced the uncles that the first strong wind would topple the structure. But his aunts kept faith in their nephew.

A few weeks after the tower was completed, a raging storm surged up from the southwest. Lightning streaked the sky and thunderclaps reverberated across The Valley. Howling gusts of wind shook buildings and barns and uprooted trees. By morning the storm had passed and with the dawn all the uncles went to their windows to peer at the hilltop, expecting to see a tangled wreckage where the tower had been. Much to their amazement, the tower stood, its wheel still whirling in the storm's last gusts. They were certain, however, that this was just a fluke. The tower could not continue to withstand the Wisconsin weather much longer. But as each storm came and went, the tower remained. It would eventually outlast them all, even its youthful designer.

The twentieth century began with the promise of revolutionary changes in the entire world's standard of living. Horseless carriages were starting to be seen on the streets of some American cities. In a bicycle repair shop in Dayton, Ohio, two brothers, Orville and Wilbur Wright, were trying to build a machine for powered flight. And in Oak Park, Illinois, Frank Lloyd Wright was designing houses and coming up with new possibilities in the field of organic architecture. Before the new century was half over, civilization would have taken greater strides forward than even these men had ever dreamed.

Tower Romeo and Juliet braving its first fierce Wisconsin storm. Few thought the tower would be able to withstand strong winds and pelting rain, but after the storm was over, the tower still stood!

When Frank Lloyd Wright was completing the Johnson Administration Building at Racine, Wisconsin, he put on a remarkable demonstration to prove the safety of his design. The now famous "lily pad" supports for the roof of the large central room were under attack from the licensing authorities. There was some doubt among the officials that the columns could support the loads they were designed to carry. Frank decided to dispel their doubts once and for all. Always the showman, he announced in the newspapers that the test would be held on a certain day. About half of the people in the crowd that showed up to witness the event felt the test would fail. The other half expressed their faith in a Wright design. Frank was there to direct the demonstration.

While police held the crowds at a safe distance, a crane placed a great load of scrap iron on the lily pad of the demonstration column. When another load was added, the crowd buzzed with excitement. The rather delicate-appearing column now held six tons—the estimated load it would have to carry in the completed building. The building code, however, required a safety factor of about four to one, so the test was not over yet. Ton after ton was added to the column as the spectators held their breath. Soon the required twenty-four tons had been exceeded and still the column stood. The crowd expected Frank to stop now, but he suddenly waved his arms at the operator and called, "Let's see how much it will hold. Keep piling it on." With that, the operator picked up another load of scrap iron and added it to the pile on the column. Another, another, and yet another ton was added. With each load the crowd held its breath in anticipation of a crash.

Finally, as the crane deposited the sixtieth ton on the lily pad, the column cracked, held for a moment, and then plunged in a tremendous roar to the ground. As the great cloud of dust settled, the architect grinned triumphantly. There would be no more trouble with the licensing authorities. Frank Lloyd Wright's building had a proven safety factor of nearly ten to one. Once again he had shown that awesome strength did not have to be achieved at the expense of architectural grace and beauty.

A Temple for Oak Park

The studio on Chicago Avenue in Oak Park was a bustling place during those first years of the new century. Despite Wright's somewhat unconventional style, his houses drew a sufficient number of admirers to keep him and his several aides and apprentices very busy. Soon there were many prairie houses scattered throughout the suburbs of Chicago and other towns in Illinois. These included the B. Harley Bradley house in Kankakee, completed in 1900, and the strikingly handsome home of Ward Willits in Highland Park, completed two years later. In keeping with his theory of organic architecture, Frank also began designing the furniture and fixtures for his houses. He readily admitted that his first efforts in furniture design did not succeed very well from the standpoint of human comfort. "I have been black and blue in some spot, somewhere, almost all of my life from too intimate contact with my own early furniture," he wrote in later years. He persisted, however, and soon his interior designs became as famous as his exterior designs.

In 1903, Frank designed a house for Mr. W. E. Martin of Oak Park. Some-

Exterior view of the Ward Willits house in Highland Park, Illinois, completed in 1902. By now, Frank was well established as an architect, and one could find many of his prairie houses around Chicago and throughout the state of Illinois.

time later, Mr. Martin's brother, Darwin, arrived from Buffalo, New York, for a visit. He was so impressed with his brother's home that he asked Frank to come to Buffalo to design one for him. The house Frank designed for Darwin Martin, also a prairie house, gave Frank Lloyd Wright exposure in Buffalo, where he eventually designed a number of homes. The Darwin Martin house remains to this day a superb example of what can result when an imaginative architect is given unrestricted freedom and financial means.

Martin was the head of the Larkin Soap Company, a Buffalo firm. He was so pleased with the house Frank designed for him that he hired the architect to design a new administrative building for his firm. Frank would later refer to this building as "the first emphatic protest in architecture . . . against the tide of meaningless elaboration sweeping the United States." Indeed, the Larkin Building was remarkable in its simplicity; Frank called it "a simple cliff of brick." It had many relatively new features, such as specially designed built-in metal furniture and air conditioning. Because it was built near railroad tracks, the building was hermetically sealed to keep out the smoke and gases from the trains. The top floor was a restaurant and the roof was designed as a recreation area. It was, no doubt, the most unusual factory office building ever constructed to that date.

Though the Larkin Building has since been destroyed, it established a precedent for the modern office building of today with its brightly-lit interior, air conditioning, and cafeteria. It was a breakthrough in the field of industrial architecture.

The ultimate masterpiece of the decade for Frank Lloyd Wright was a Unitarian church, the Unity Temple, in his hometown of Oak Park. In June of

Unity Temple in Oak Park, Illinois. This Unitarian church was devoid of the traditional religious symbols; it also was one of the first large buildings to be constructed entirely of concrete.

1904, the old wooden church burned to the ground. A building committee was formed to plan and arrange for a new church. Mr. Charles E. Roberts, an engineer who was one of the committee members, recommended that Frank be commissioned to design the new building. His design made architectural history.

Traditionally, churches had been designed with considerable religious symbolism. Towering spires and steeples, for example, are symbolic fingers pointing to heaven. In considering how a church should look, Frank was concerned more with the human sensibilities involved than he was with symbols, which he thought to be too literal. He wanted to design a temple that in itself could create a sense of the unity of God and man. He did not want a design that said explicitly "this is a church," yet failed to give the beholder a "sense of inner rhythm." It would be a "natural building"—organic architecture whose total design could not be complete without the presence of man and the spirit of God.

The design that ultimately evolved was a cubic mass of gray concrete, elegant in its clean simplicity. Because the site was close to busy streets and trolley tracks, the church has heavy walls to keep out the sounds of the city. The auditorium, as the main room of worship was called, is reached through passageways leading from a central foyer. Stairways at each corner of the building lead from the passageways up to the skylit auditorium which has a seating capacity of four hundred. Frank wanted anyone emerging from the dark corridors to the brightness of the auditorium to have a spiritual, almost magical, experience.

Apart from its somewhat radical departure from traditional church design, an outstanding feature of the Unity Temple was the choice of material for its construction. Concrete is an ancient material dating back at least to the Romans and Greeks. Frank Lloyd Wright's Unity Temple, however, was one of the first large buildings to be constructed entirely of concrete. The spectacular results in Oak Park proved to others what could be done with this material, and opened almost unlimited possibilities in modern architecture. Unity Temple was a convincing demonstration that reinforced concrete could be used both for ornamentation and for the load-carrying parts of a structure. The modern style of architecture that we know today, with its crisp, uncluttered lines, would be very difficult to execute without concrete.

The completed building included Unity House, with classrooms for study, a large hall for banquets, and a kitchen. This lesser building is connected to the main one by the entrance foyer and pastor's study. It, too, is of clean, geometric lines, devoid of façade or ornamentation. The two parts of the building blended in perfect harmony.

Unity Temple was opened in 1907. The resulting wide publicity brought comments from around the world and thousands of curious sightseers to Oak Park. As expected, reaction to this radical new design was mixed. The Victorian era of gabled, turreted houses with elaborate ornamentation was just ending, yet many people simply were not ready to accept modern architecture as anything more than a fad. Consequently, the design of Unity Temple drew tremendous outcries of criticism. But it had many admirers, too, and the Unitarian Church of Oak Park would go down in history as one of the most famous and remarkable works of Frank Lloyd Wright.

Wright was now swamped with commissions for other work. In 1908 he designed what he has called his "most successful" dwelling, for Mr. and Mrs. Avery Coonley at Riverside, Illinois. This house, with its furniture, fixtures,

---

Two views of the Avery Coonley house, one of Frank Lloyd Wright's most beautiful homes, completed in 1908 at Riverside, Illinois. Top, the pool and back of the house. Bottom, view from the front walkway.

and reflecting pool all designed by Wright, was indeed among his greatest achievements.

The following year, Wright designed a house for Mr. Frederick C. Robie. Unlike the other prairie houses, the Robie house was built in the city of Chicago not far from the University of Chicago campus. This handsome brick mansion was saved from the wreckers' iron ball in recent years by a real estate developer who wished to preserve this classic example of Frank Lloyd Wright's design.

As the commissions poured in, Frank had to put in more and more hours at his drawing board in the studio. "I was losing grip on my work and even interest in it," he remembered later. "Every day of every week and far into the night of nearly every day, Sunday included, I had 'added tired to tired' and added it again and yet again, as I had been trained to do by Uncle James on the farm as a boy." The terrific pace was beginning to tell. He had little time left for his family. There were six children now (Llewellyn was born in 1905), and Catherine had to assume more and more of the responsibility for their upbringing. The strain began to tell on her, too, and soon the love which had burned so brightly between them began to fade. One day in the fall of 1909, after nearly twenty years of marriage, Frank left his family and never returned to the house in Oak Park.

As the first decade of the twentieth century ended, so ended a phase of the career of Frank Lloyd Wright. He had reached a pinnacle of success in his career, and the path now began to take a downward turn. For the next two decades or more he would face trials and tribulations terrible enough to ruin most men. But the genius of Frank Lloyd Wright was not to be denied. He would emerge again from near ruin to leave his name at the very peak of architectural history.

The Frederick C. Robie house, located in Chicago near the University of Chicago campus and designed in 1909. This house differed from most prairie houses in that it was located right in the city of Chicago.

Taliesin, Tragedy, and Tokyo

Frank Lloyd Wright was on the verge of a nervous breakdown from overwork when he left Oak Park and his family. He felt that a vacation was now absolutely necessary. Turning over his unfinished work to his subordinates, he took a train to New York and then sailed to Europe.

As the ship coursed its way across the stormy North Atlantic, Frank had time to relax and consider his plans for the future. He knew that he would not return to his family, and felt that he needed a fresh start, in a new place, under new conditions. He would, of course, continue to provide for his family, and all the children would go to either colleges or universities. But the marriage was ended and the once happy family would never again be a complete unit.

Ernst Wasmuth, an art publisher in Berlin, Germany, wanted to publish a special illustrated portfolio devoted entirely to Wright's works. The architect had readily given his permission and now decided to begin his vacation by going to the lovely old German capital city to help in the portfolio's preparation. The resulting publication was the first major exposure Europeans had to Frank's ideas of "organic architecture." It was to have a significant impact and influence on European architecture in the years that followed. Frank stayed in Europe nearly a year, spending con-

---

Here we see Frank working on one of the many assignments he took on during the years in Oak Park. Eventually the strain began to tell on his relations with his family, and he found himself forced to leave them.

siderable time in Italy studying various periods of Roman and Italian architecture. By the time he returned to America in 1910, he had a plan for his future.

Often over the years, Frank's thoughts had turned to The Valley and the beautiful landscape he knew and loved so well. Upon his return, his mother gave him the two hundred acres of land that she had inherited from the estate of her father, Richard Lloyd-Jones. Here, rested and revived, Frank thought he would be able to find the freedom, peace, and quiet he so longed for. He decided to begin his new life in The Valley.

There had to be a home, of course, and a studio and other buildings. Frank immediately set to work drawing a design he had carried in his mind for a long while. He fashioned a creation of wood and stone which took its form and substance from the landscape and which would use rock from a nearby quarry. In his ancestral land in the rolling hills of Wisconsin, the master architect created what many feel is his greatest masterpiece. He called it "Taliesin."

The name Taliesin is taken from the Welsh poet of the same name, but literally translated it means "shining brow." Taliesin was never completed in a final form. Perhaps Wright never intended it to be. He was constantly making alterations—changing a building here, adding a wall there. From the very beginning, he planned it to be a considerable undertaking.

"Taliesin," he wrote later, "was to be an architect's workshop, a dwelling as well for young workers who came to assist. And it was a farm cottage for the farm help . . . The place was to be self-sustaining if not self-sufficient and with

Taliesin I, Frank's house in Wisconsin which was destroyed by fire in 1914. Frank had planned Taliesin to be a retreat for himself from the pressures of his work and from the hustle and bustle of Chicago.

its domain of two hundred acres, shelter, food, clothes, and even entertainment within itself. It had to be its own light-plant, fuelyard, transportation and water system."

Frank also had a vision of the future of Taliesin. It was to be a "recreation ground for my children and their children perhaps for many generations more." With this dream in mind, and the comforting scenery of The Valley to inspire him, "Gradually creative desire and faith came creeping back again. Taliesin began to come alive and settle down to work."

Frank maintained an office in Chicago along with a small apartment. During most of each week he remained in the city, but he was always anxious to hurry home to his beloved Taliesin on Friday afternoons. At last he had a sanctuary to which he could retreat, leaving behind the cares and problems of the city. Taliesin was a bustling place, filled with workmen, assistant architects, gardeners, stonemasons, and carpenters. All were handpicked by Wright, and all shared a common enthusiasm for the throbbing, living enterprise that was Taliesin. Here was a beautiful little world in which all inhabitants lived and worked in communal harmony.

In 1913, a major commission came to Frank Lloyd Wright—the design of the Midway Gardens on Chicago's South Side. This was to be an outdoor garden for dining, concerts, and other entertainment. Because of the short summer season in the "Windy City," a winter garden was also planned. Midway Gardens was to be a unique addition to the social life of Chicago, reminiscent of the old Bavarian beer gardens in Germany.

Midway Gardens on Chicago's South Side, completed in 1914. This was planned as a complex in which performances such as concerts could be held year-round—outdoors in summer and indoors in winter.

Frank's designs were submitted and accepted and work quietly began. By the summer of 1914, the Midway Gardens were nearing completion. But this was to be a tragic summer. War, which would soon involve most of the nations of the world, erupted in Europe. A deep personal tragedy was also to befall Frank Lloyd Wright.

On August 15, Frank and his son John, who had become an apprentice architect serving under his father, were having lunch in the nearly completed dining room at Midway Gardens when there was a long-distance telephone call for Frank. There had been a tragedy at Taliesin—could he come at once? John and Frank caught the first available train for Wisconsin. At Spring Green they were told the terrible news.

At lunchtime on this fateful day, six of the Taliesin employees were eating in the staff dining room. They included two draftsmen, two handymen, and Mr. William Weston and his thirteen-year-old son, Ernest. Weston was a carpenter and Frank's "right-hand man" at Taliesin. On the terrace nearby, Mrs. Mamah Borthwick Cheney and her two children, who were guests of Wright's, were also having lunch. The meal was being served by Julian Carleton, a man from

Barbados who had been the cook at Taliesin since early summer. Suddenly, Carleton went berserk. The quiet scene on this beautiful August day was shattered by an explosion and fire, purposely set by Carleton.

As the six employees ran out of the dining room, their clothes ablaze, Carleton appeared with an ax. Before anyone could understand what was happening, the madman had struck them all down. Then he had raced out to the terrace and killed Mrs. Cheney and her children. Only William Weston and one of the draftsmen, both of them burned and wounded, managed to escape. Meanwhile, Frank Lloyd Wright's beloved Taliesin burned to the ground. The murderer then swallowed poison and died several days later without ever uttering a word.

When he arrived, Wright saw only a terrible blackened ruin—all that remained of Taliesin. The full significance of the horror—seven lives snuffed out in a few shattering moments—plunged Frank into the darkest depths of despair. "From the moment of my return to that devastating scene of horror I had wanted to see no one," he recalled later. "The nights were filled with strange unreasoning terror. No moon

---

Julian Carleton, a cook at Taliesin, set Frank's beloved home afire and killed seven people one horrible day in August, 1914. Frank arrived from Chicago stricken with sadness at the sight of what had happened. He was unable to throw off his despondency for a long while, but knew that a new Taliesin must "rise from the ashes."

seemed to shine. No stars in the sky . . . Strange, unnatural silence, the smoke still rising from certain portions of the ruin . . . A kind of black despair seemed to paralyze my imagination . . . numbed my sensibilities . . . the blow was too severe."

Many men would not have been able to recover from so great a tragedy. Memories and terrible anguish can permanently dampen the creativity, the will, and the spirit of a man. But Frank Lloyd Wright was no ordinary man. "There is release from anguish in action," he said. "Anguish would not leave Taliesin until action for renewal began. There was to be no turning back nor stopping to mourn. What had been beautiful at Taliesin should live as a grateful memory creating the new. Steadily, again, stone by stone, board by board, Taliesin II began to rise from the ashes of Taliesin the first."

Work progressed rapidly on Taliesin II as Frank poured his energies into the task in an effort to forget the tragedy. The design of the new Taliesin took a different shape from the old. As Wright worked to improve this example of organic architecture he gave Taliesin II a touch of the Oriental.

The year before, Frank had met a Japanese delegation in New York who were searching for an American architect to design a new Imperial Hotel in Tokyo. In the fall of 1915, a Mr. Hayashi came to Taliesin to look at sketches Frank had made for the proposed hotel. Mr. Hayashi was pleased, and on his recommendation, Frank was given the commission. In the spring of 1916 Frank sailed to Japan to begin the work.

During the next six years, from 1916 to 1922, Frank spent much of his time in Tokyo where he lived in the old Imperial Hotel while the mighty new "Impeho" was being built. He did make several trips to America where he visited Taliesin and also began to develop a business in southern California, but most of Frank's work at this time involved the Imperial Hotel.

It was an immense undertaking, certainly the largest Frank had attempted up to that time. There were many unique problems, two of these being earthquakes and the language barrier.

Japan has always been plagued with earthquakes because it is located within a well-defined earthquake region. The biggest problem for the architect was to

---

The Imperial Hotel in Tokyo, Japan, which Frank designed in 1916-1922. It was especially designed to withstand earthquakes, for Japan is located in an earthquake region. It was also the largest structure Frank had built up to that time.

design a building that was earthquake-proof. Frank first discovered that below an eight-foot layer of surface soil lay some sixty to seventy feet of soft mud. This, he decided, would make an excellent cushion to absorb the shock of earthquakes. He would also make the building flexible by linking parts of the structure with joints. Frank compared the cantilevers supporting thc floors to "a waiter carrying his tray on upraised arm and fingers at the center—*balancing* the load." He had faith that his design would withstand any earthquake.

Because of the language barrier, Frank could not easily make clear to the workers what he wanted done. The Japanese insisted on using the ancient methods of construction—involving mostly manpower rather than western-style machinery. Here again, the language problem arose, for Frank could not make clear why machinery was better. However, the building was at last completed in 1922. Baron Okura, the chairman of the organization that owned the hotel, gave a great party in honor of the architect, and then Frank sailed home.

The next year, on September 1, 1923, a news flash crackled around the world. An earthquake had rocked Japan and first reports said that Tokyo and Yokohama had both been completely destroyed. Frank's major concern was whether or not his hotel had survived the quake, as it had been designed to do. Days passed and still Frank could get no definite news. Casualty figures rose, and ultimately 74,000 were reported dead. More than fifty percent of all the brick buildings in the city of Tokyo came down and some 700,000 other dwellings were burned in the fire that followed. It was the most devastating earthquake in history.

Frank's concern was relieved on September 13—nearly two weeks after the disaster—when he received the following telegram:

> HOTEL STANDS UNDAMAGED AS MONUMENT OF YOUR GENIUS. HUNDREDS OF HOMELESS PROVIDED BY PERFECTLY MAINTAINED SERVICE.
> CONGRATULATIONS
> OKURA

In November of 1923, Frank Lloyd Wright married for the second time. He had met his new wife, Miriam Noel, shortly after the tragedy at Taliesin ten years before. She was a divorcée with grown children who had spent part of her life in Europe. Unfortunately, the marriage was destined to be a turbulent affair that would bring new pressures and troubles to the fifty-four-year-old architect. In fact, the couple parted almost as soon as the marriage began.

The Imperial Hotel during one of Japan's famous earthquakes. The efficacy of Frank's design was admirably demonstrated when this building was one of the few left intact after the quake; Frank received a congratulatory telegram from the hotel's owner.

At almost the same time that his marriage to Miriam Noel dissolved, Frank's career took another downward plunge. Commissions became scarce and Frank was constantly harrassed by debt collectors. Then another tragedy—Taliesin II burned to the ground one night in 1925. With little money, and no immediate prospect of earning any more, Frank slowly began building Taliesin III and lived in what he had been able to salvage of the Taliesin II ruin.

These were lean, hard years for Frank Lloyd Wright. But as the "Roaring Twenties" ended and America began its plunge into economic depression, Frank took a step that would mark a new upward turn in his life. This step had nothing to do with architecture, as such, but it would greatly affect his happiness, his contentment, and his peace of mind. And in so doing it would rekindle the creative desire and stimulate the genius so long suppressed by despair. At Rancho Santa Fe, near La Jolla, California, Frank married for the third and final time—one year after he had finally managed to obtain a divorce from Miriam. His bride, Olgivanna, was to provide Frank with the inspiration, the help, the comfort, and the love he needed as he established himself once and for all as the greatest living American architect.

Taliesin III, begun in the late 1920's on the site of Taliesin I and II, in The Valley. When this project was begun, Frank was going through grave financial and emotional problems, but nothing could stop him from rebuilding his beloved Taliesin.

Left, an interior shot of Taliesin III. Right, Frank Lloyd Wright stands on a hillside in Wisconsin near Taliesin, surveying his domain.

The Last Climb to the Top

Frank had met Olga Iovanova Lazovich Milanoff Hinsenberg at a concert in Chicago. Olgivanna, as she was called, was from the little Balkan country of Montenegro, which had become a part of the new nation of Yugoslavia following World War I. She also was a divorcée, and had a little girl named Svetlana. It was love at first sight for Frank and the dark-haired beauty with the quiet and elegant manner. Together they would share more than three decades of happiness.

Soon after their marriage, Frank and Olgivanna returned to Taliesin from California. The place was very run-down after having been vacant for several months, and there was little money with which to put it in good order. In fact, a bank in Madison had been holding Taliesin against a long overdue note. In an effort to obtain money to pay his debts, Frank had taken the unusual step of selling shares of himself as a corporation. What it really amounted to, of course, was that friends were loaning him money in a very legal way. Some $75,000 was obtained in this fashion, which is a revealing testimony to the faith many people had in the honesty and earning power of Frank Lloyd Wright even at the nadir of his career. The money was quickly used, however, partly to fight lawsuits brought against him by his second wife, Miriam Noel Wright, and partly to pay outstanding debts. "The next move, the next meal," he said, "is becoming a problem to be solved without money. There is less than none."

In the late summer of 1932, as Franklin D. Roosevelt campaigned for the presidency to the tune of "Happy Days are Here Again," Frank set up a school for young architects, calling it the Taliesin Fellowship. This school boasted a rather unusual curriculum. Students were expected to participate in all facets of life at Taliesin including gardening, driving a farm tractor, cooking in the kitchen, serving dinner, chopping trees, and doing any other jobs necessary to sustain the little community. Frank felt that mere classroom instruction could not give an apprentice a true feeling for organic architecture; he wanted them to sense creativity in and unity with nature. Students came from around the world to join in this enterprise. A few of them dropped out after a short time when they discovered they would have to take their turn doing menial tasks. Those who stayed on—some for as long as twenty years—received a thorough background in organic architecture. Not only did they learn to understand Wright's concepts and methods, they gained valuable experience in the prac-

---

Frank Lloyd Wright suffered many setbacks throughout his career, such as the fires at Taliesin and the many lawsuits brought by his second wife, Miriam Noel Wright. Yet, he managed to rise above all of these problems to become the greatest American architect of the first half of the twentieth century.

The eighth of June—Mr. Wright's birthday—was always an important day at Taliesin. The students and apprentices were present, as well as visiting guests. Respect and affection were expressed with the usual gifts and flowers, followed by a party with fine food and music. There was one tradition at Taliesin, however, that made the celebration of Mr. Wright's birthday unique. This was the presentation of the "Birthday Box." The Birthday Box was designed and built each year especially for the occasion. Each was beautifully made by an apprentice eager to outshine past box designers. This handsome work of art was presented to the architect as part of the birthday celebration. The box was filled with projects completed by each of the students. Some were architectural drawings or plans. Others were paintings or models. Many were handcrafted artworks of ceramic or textiles. All were the best work of the individuals who made them.

As the young apprentices gathered around the master's chair, he would study each item and comment about its merit and offer kindly advice or criticism. This was followed by an open discussion among the students before Mr. Wright went on to the next gift. These discussions were really lectures in art, especially architectural art, by the master of them all.

Frank Lloyd Wright was happiest when he was surrounded by young people. They represented the hope for the future. Wright himself retained a youthful spirit throughout his whole life. Every year on his birthday that spirit seemed to be re-emphasized when, surrounded by his young apprentices, he received the traditional Birthday Box.

tical aspects of building: carpentry, electrical wiring, plumbing, masonry, and house painting.

The Fellowship was meant to encourage not only architecture, but all forms of art. There were competitions in oil painting, watercolors, and sketching, with the prize usually little more than the accolades of fellow students. Olgivanna led discussions in philosophy and literature as well as serving as housemother, financial manager, and kitchen overseer. Her tireless efforts from dawn to dusk earned her the love and affection of all the students. The students staged their own entertainments with music and dancing, often writing their own musical scores for little stage productions. Later, a little theater was built where movies were shown once a week. Above all, Frank wanted the apprentices to learn to "add tired to tired." They did, and in a most delightful way.

Of course Taliesin was not an accredited college as such. The only "diploma" given in the Taliesin Fellowship was a personal testimonial from Frank Lloyd Wright. Nonetheless, as the years progressed, the men and women who had served their apprenticeship at Taliesin were in great demand in the field of architecture.

Wright did not inaugurate the Fellowship to make money, and though he charged an annual fee of $1100 per student at Taliesin, he would waive all or part of it if he felt that an apprentice who could not afford the tuition was worth retaining. To supplement this rather meager income, for expenses at Taliesin were high, Frank began to write books and magazine articles. During the middle 1930's, Wright was also in demand throughout the world as a lecturer. He and Mrs. Wright made a trip to Brazil when Frank was invited there to judge a competition for a Columbus memorial. Gradually life began to get better for the energetic architect and his loyal wife.

During the last half of the 1930's, Frank surged back to the forefront of American architecture. In 1936, he designed what has often been described

Student life at Taliesin. Above, the students "add tired to tired" by doing manual chores. Top right, a concert given by some of the students. Mr. and Mrs. Wright are seated in front of the piano. Bottom right, students gather around Mr. Wright as he explains a fine point of architecture.

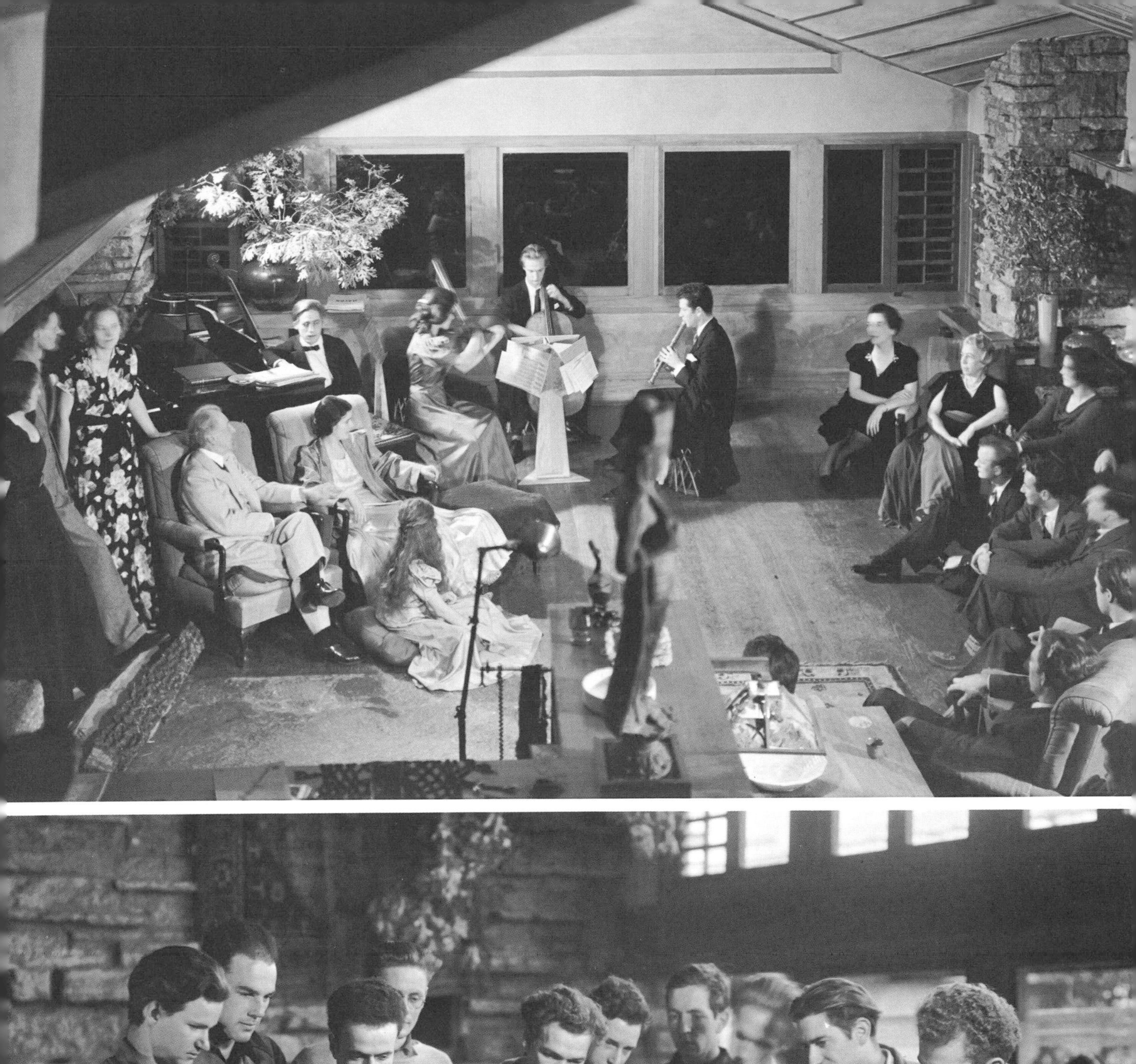

as the most beautiful dwelling in the world—at Bear Run, Pennsylvania, near Pittsburgh. "Falling Water," as the house is called, is a handsome blending of native rock and concrete. It nestles among the trees in a little vale, with a bubbling mountain stream running right through the house. It fits so beautifully into its natural surroundings that it can be called the ultimate in organic architecture.

In that same year Frank began work on the Johnson Wax administration building at Racine, Wisconsin. Completed in 1939, it is one of the most remarkable buildings of its kind in America. The "lily pad" roof supports —like so many other Wright innovations, thought at first to be impractical and unsuited for their stated purpose—have become famous around the world. In later years Frank was commissioned to design the Johnson Research Tower for the same company and a home called "Wingspread," for a member of the Johnson family.

Before the decade had ended, honors and official recognition were making the name Frank Lloyd Wright more famous than ever. In 1938, the prestigious magazine *Architectural Forum* devoted an entire issue to his work. The following year he went to England where he delivered a series of lectures and received the Royal Gold Medal from the Royal Institute of British Architects. Other honors would follow with increasing frequency for the rest of his life.

It was during this same period that Frank designed and built his now-famous Taliesin West on Maricopa Mesa near Scottsdale, Arizona. This striking complex served as a winter residence for the Wrights and their students. The desert environment contrasts sharply with the rolling hills near Spring Green, Wisconsin, and the Wrights and their apprentices eagerly looked forward to the change of scene—Wisconsin in the spring and Arizona in the fall. The children, Svetlana and Iovanna (Frank and Olgivanna's own daughter), also looked forward to the trips in one of Frank's many automobiles. With the growth of commercial aviation after World War II, Frank and Olgivanna usually flew, while students drove the cars.

During the 1940's, Frank designed several buildings for Florida Southern College. His buildings, especially Pfeiffer Chapel, make the campus of this little college at Lakeland, Florida, one of the most renowned in America. Another of his famous buildings of that period is the V. C. Morris Gift Shop, on Maiden Lane in San Francisco, California.

Frank Lloyd Wright celebrated his eightieth birthday in 1949, but he looked and acted thirty years younger. His hair, which he still wore in his own distinctive style, was now snow-white. But there was still a spring to his step and he carried his cane as a sort of non-military swagger stick.

If his appearance was younger than his years, his heart was younger still. He had complete faith in the youth of America and was rarely happier than when surrounded by young people. He even commented once that high school students should be the ones to choose designs for municipal buildings. One day he received a letter from a little girl who asked him to design a house for her pet dog. With a delighted chuckle he went immediately to his drawing board and in short order drew a plan that would satisfy the most discriminating canine taste. In a few days the youngster received the design, complete with the Frank Lloyd Wright signature and his personal symbol, a red square, which he usually added to his drawings.

During the last decade of his life, Frank Lloyd Wright became one of the

---

Two photographs of Frank Lloyd Wright's later houses. Top left, Falling Water, located in Bear Run, Pennsylvania. This house has a stream running right through it. Bottom left, a model of Wingspread, the home of Herbert Johnson at Racine, Wisconsin.

Three photographs of Taliesin West, located on the Maricopa Mesa in Arizona. Top left, an exterior view. Bottom left, the driveway. Right, the fountain.

WESTERN
UNION

best-known men in America. Wherever he went, newspapermen and photographers were at his heels, for he was always ready with a newsworthy comment. Invariably he was asked his opinion of new buildings designed by other architects. If he liked the design he gave it lavish praise which he expressed with great eloquence. If, however, he did not like the design, his now-famed caustic wit could reduce what others might consider a fine piece of architecture to the rank of "General Grant Gothic" or some other equally descriptive title expressing his displeasure.

He was frequently asked the question, "Mr. Wright, which do you consider the greatest of your buildings?"

His stock answer was proof of his ever-youthful spirit: "The next one," he would say, "always the next one."

In 1956, Frank startled America with his design for a city-within-a-building which he called Mile High Illinois. The plan called for a colossal structure of 528 stories which would dwarf the 102-story Empire State Building in New York. No building plans have been made so far, since the cost of construction would, of course, be extremely high. But the plans are all drawn and perhaps someday in the future someone will convince the world that Mile High Illinois is one answer to the population explosion.

Frank completed many designs during the 1950's. Though they could not rival the originality of his Mile High plan, they caused Americans to shake their heads in wonderment at the clear thinking and seemingly boundless energy of a man approaching his ninetieth birthday. Among these was the First Unitarian Meeting House in Madison, Wisconsin, and the H. C. Price Tower in Bartlesville, Oklahoma. There were handsome dwellings in such distant places as Carmel-By-The-Sea, California, and Quasqueton, Iowa. And finally there was the Solomon R. Guggenheim Museum on Fifth Avenue in New York City—certainly one of Wright's most well-known buildings.

Early in 1959, Wright made a journey to New York to watch as workmen put the final touches on the Guggenheim Museum. He was sprightly and gay, posing with a twinkling smile for a group of young artists with cameras. Later, he returned to the warm Arizona sun and his drawing board at Taliesin West. Several weeks passed in happy, busy activity and then on the fourth of April, he was stricken with abdominal pains and taken to a hospital in Phoenix. The doctors operated on him, and for awhile it seemed that the grand old man would recover. Then, early on the morning of April 9, 1959, Frank Lloyd Wright quietly passed away in his sleep. After eighty-nine years and ten months, the roller-coaster life and career of Frank Lloyd Wright was over. He was buried in the Lloyd-Jones family cemetery at Spring Green, Wisconsin.

Many of Frank Lloyd Wright's earlier buildings have been torn down, but America is still dotted with several hundred of his structures, each standing as a mute testimonial to his creative genius. These, in themselves, would assure Frank Lloyd Wright a place in history. But it was his idea of creating a distinctively American architecture, and especially the acceptance of his ideas by the American public and by his fellow architects, that remains as his greatest monument. More than any other architect, Frank Lloyd Wright gave his nation and his time an architectural styling distinctively their own.

Frank Lloyd Wright was active up until his death at age 90. Top, Wright discusses the design for the H. C. Price Tower in Oklahoma with the director of the Solomon R. Guggenheim Museum in New York. Bottom, Wright with a model of the Guggenheim Museum.

Summary

Frank Lloyd Wright was one of those rare individuals who know at a very early age the profession they will take as their lifework. It is said that even before his birth his mother had dreamed of having a son who would become an architect. Why she chose this field has never been explained. It is certain, however, that she encouraged her son's seemingly natural interest in architecture. Even before he started to school, young Frank developed an awareness of natural forms. He amassed a collection of stones, not from an interest in geology but from an interest in their never-ending variety of shapes. Later, his mother bought him a set of Froebel blocks that gave the boy a sense of geometric form and dimension.

It is said that Frank announced on his ninth birthday that he would grow up to be the greatest architect in the world. Whether this story is fact or fiction is unimportant. What is significant is that many people qualified to make a judgment have stated that he did indeed live up to this prediction.

Wright had the good fortune to serve his apprenticeship under Louis Sullivan, one of the pioneers of modern architecture. This great architect, whom Wright always called *Lieber Meister* (Dear Master), took the first steps away from traditional styling in architecture. It was Frank Lloyd Wright, however, who carried on where Sullivan had left off. It was he who stood as a rallying point for the increasing number of young "radicals" who shared his views and recognized his genius.

During his career, which spanned seven decades, Wright produced more than seven hundred churches, houses, schools, theaters, museums, stores, and office buildings. Each of these was an original, designed exactly for its purpose and location, and coming directly from the mind and heart of Frank Lloyd Wright.

Each of his designs expressed, to some degree, his theme of "organic architecture": that a building should be *of* its natural surroundings, rather than built *on* them. He thought in terms of "organic simplicity" and threw out excessive ornamentation. He waged a ceaseless war against "the box," as he called the little square rooms within a square house, so popular in turn-of-the-century architecture. In developing new techniques and working with new materials he achieved plasticity of form.

For many years he was considered a radical, even a heretic, and his business suffered. Had he wished to follow traditional architectural styling and a more conventional way of life, Frank Lloyd Wright could have become a very wealthy man. But he remained ever loyal to his concepts, and would not compromise his principles for the sake of making money.

Far ahead of his time in the early days of his career, he lived a long and busy life, and before he died witnessed the acceptance of his ideas by his profession, his country, and the world. More than any other architect, Frank Lloyd Wright gave to the twentieth century a distinctive style of its own.

Bibliography

BLAKE, PETER. *The Master Builder*. New York: Alfred A. Knopf, 1960.

DREXLER, ARTHUR. *The Drawings of Frank Lloyd Wright*. New York: Horizon Press, 1962.

FARR, FINIS. *Frank Lloyd Wright*. New York: Scribner's, 1961.

FORSEE, AYLESA. *Frank Lloyd Wright, Rebel in Concrete*. Philadelphia: Macrae Smith, 1959.

GUTHEIM, FREDERICK, ed. *Frank Lloyd Wright on Architecture: Selected Writings*. New York: Duell, Sloan & Pearce, 1941.

HAMLIN, TALBOT. *Architecture Through the Ages*. New York: G. P. Putnam's, 1953.

HITCHCOCK, HENRY. *In the Nature of Materials; The Buildings of Frank Lloyd Wright*. New York: Duell, Sloan & Pearce, 1942.

HOUSE BEAUTIFUL SPECIAL ISSUE. *Frank Lloyd Wright, his contributions to the beauty of American life* (includes a bibliography). New York: November, 1955.

KAUFMAN, EDGAR and BEN RAEBURN. *Writings and Buildings, 1941* (collected lectures and magazine articles by Wright).

KEY, ELLEN. *Love and Ethics* (translated by Mamah Bouton Borthwick and Frank Lloyd Wright). Chicago: The Ralph Fletcher Seymour Company, 1912.

MANSON, GRANT. *Frank Lloyd Wright to 1910*. New York: Reinhold, 1958.

SARGEANT, WINTHROP. *Geniuses, Goddesses and People*. New York: Dutton, 1949.

SCULLY, VINCENT. *Frank Lloyd Wright*. New York: Braziller, 1960.

VEVI, BRUNO. *Towards an Organic Architecture*. London: Faber & Faber, 1950.

WRIGHT, FRANK LLOYD. *An Autobiography*. New York: Duell, Sloan & Pearce, 1943.

———. *An Organic Adventure: The Architecture of Democracy*, 1939.

———. *A Testament*. New York: Horizon Press, 1957.

———. *Drawings for a Living Architecture*. New York: Horizon Press, 1959.

———. *Genius and the Mobocracy*, 1949.

———. *Modern Architecture*, 1931.

———. *The Future of Architecture*, 1953.

———. *The Disappearing City*, 1932.

———. *The Natural House*, 1954.

———. *The Story of the Tower: The Tree That Escaped the Crowded Forest*, 1956.

———. *Two Lectures on Architecture*. Chicago: The Art Institute of Chicago, 1931.

———. *When Democracy Builds*, 1945.

———. with Baker Brownell. *Architecture and Modern Life*, 1937.

WRIGHT, IOVANNA. *Architecture: Man in Possession of his Earth*. New York: Doubleday, 1962.

WRIGHT, JOHN LLOYD. *My Father Who Is On Earth*. New York: Putnam's, 1946.

WRIGHT, OLGIVANNA. *The Shining Brow*. New York: Horizon Press, 1960.

———. *Our House*. New York: Horizon Press, 1959.

Index

Acknowledgments: Photographs on pages 2-3, 79, 84, 88, and 90 from the files of Wide World Photos, Inc.; photographs on pages 10, 37, 44, 54-55, 57, 59, 61, 66-67, and 70 from the files of Chicago Architectural Photographing Co.; photographs on pages 40, 75, 76, 77, 83, 86, and 87 from the files of Hedrich-Blessing; photograph on page 31 from the files of Historical Pictures Service. Illustrations on pages 8, 13, 15, 17, 19, 21, 22-23, 25, 27, 29, 33, 34, 39, 43, 47, 49, 51, 52-53, 62, 65, 69, 72, 80-81, and 82 by Harley Shelton, Hollis Associates.